Think Yourself Loved

Also by Debbie Johnson

Think Yourself Thin

How to Make Your Dreams Come True

DEBBIE JOHNSON

Unity House

Unity Village, Missouri

To receive a catalog of all our Unity publications (books, cassettes, compact discs, and magazines) or to place an order, call the Customer Service Department: (816) 969-2069 or 1-800-669-0282.

The publisher wishes to acknowledge the editorial work of Raymond Teague and Michael Maday; the copy services of Tom Lewin, Shari Behr, and Deborah Dribben; the production help of Rozanne Devine and Jane Blackwood; and the marketing efforts of Allen Liles, Jenee Meyer, and Sharon Sartin.

Cover design by Gail Ishmael.
Cover photo by Ken Clark.

Library of Congress Cataloging-in-Publication Data

Johnson, Debbie, 1951–
    Think yourself loved / Debbie Johnson. — 1st ed.
      p. cm.
    Includes bibliographical references (p.   ).
    ISBN 0-87159-242-8 (pbk.)
    1. Love—Religious aspects—Unity School of Christianity.
    2. Unity School of Christianity—Doctrines.   I. Title.
    BX9890.U505J64 1999
    241'.4—dc21   99-19430
                                            CIP

Canada BN 13252 9033 RT

Dedication

To every soul who places love above all else

Acknowledgments

TO ALL OF YOU READERS who have written and called to let me know when you have gotten help or solace from the words I write: Hearing from you is what makes my writing time worth it!

To my dear husband Myron for his encouragement, love, and patience as I worked on this labor of love, I give many thanks. Also, I am grateful for his patience and understanding as I continually work on loving myself more, so I have more to give.

To Kimberly Young, Tim Young, Mark Morrison, Carol Polevoy, and Carol Tocher, I thank you for your financial and moral support, love, and encouragement.

To Jocelyn Parrish-Nichols and Suzie Reeb, I give warm thanks for a great job of reading and editing the initial drafts of this book and others, and for being dear friends who encourage others to take good care of themselves.

To Mary Caroll Moore, Linda Anderson, and Beverly Foster, I give thanks for helping me become a better writer through suggestions, teaching, and editing.

To David Gillin, my good friend at *Evening Magazine* (KING-TV) in Seattle and a great reporter, who gave me a super start with his generosity and encouragement, I give thanks.

To Andy Welchel at the National Writers Association, I bow in humble submission to your greatness as a comedian, second only to your ability to keep me sane during the process of selling this book. Thanks also for your encouragement.

To all the bookstores who believed my little booklet *How to Love Yourself So Others Can Love You More* (upon which this book is based) could sell (or didn't believe it and tried it anyway)—thank you, you are all wonderful!

To my editor at Unity House, Raymond Teague, the kind, respectful, and open-hearted editor I waited three years to find, I give thanks!

And the biggest thank you of all goes to God, for the greatest love there is.

Table of Contents

Preface

WHAT DOES IT MEAN TO "think yourself loved"?

Thinking yourself loved means using your divine gift of imagination to bring more love into your life. Imagine that you are loved, and you are!

You're not making up something that doesn't exist, though. You are simply becoming aware of what is already present, but which you have not previously seen. You do this through envisioning or picturing or thinking—they're all the same. In other words, use all your senses and thoughts to form a mental image of the love you want in your life. The love is there waiting for you.

It sound's simple doesn't it?

Is it really that easy?

Thinking yourself loved is a process. It's not difficult; it just takes time. Begin with a decision to change your thoughts. Then, with some simple effort on your part, a change in your life will follow.

We often begin looking for love everywhere except where it resides eternally—within our true spiritual Selves. We can unlock this mysterious door to what may seem an unlikely place for love with a simple key: our divine gift of imagination.

By using your imaging-thinking ability, you can discover how to fill yourself and fill your life with love. You can find and challenge every block to accepting love, and learn to keep your heart open to all the love that surrounds you.

The true stories and exercises in this book give you the tools to take the spiritual, mental, emotional, and physical steps to bring more love into your life. The principles and ideas presented can help you find the lasting love you have always wanted and overcome the blocks to receiving it.

The greatest gift you can give God and yourself is learning to receive more of God's love, thus having more divine love to give to others.

My heart is with you on this journey. Thinking myself loved has been a long process, but I hope what I've learned will shorten the process quite a bit for you.

Here's to your readiness, and may love fill your life as it has mine!

CHAPTER 1

Tapping Into Divine Love

WHAT IS THE ONE THING that every single person in this whole wide world needs *and* wants? Of course, we *all* know it's love. Personal ads from lonely hearts are filling pages and pages in the newspapers, and dating services abound. Nightclubs are jam-packed with people hoping to meet someone special. How do I know this? From painful, personal experience.

After stuffing myself with cookies, I used to watch television and go to bed alone, again. Then I would often cry myself to sleep for the want of someone to hold me and make me feel loved, secure, and cared for.

When I woke up hoping there would magically be someone there to kiss me good morning, I was sadly disappointed.

Going to nightclubs, dance clubs, and dating clubs didn't seem to bring me the right partner. I attracted men who were exciting, but certainly not thoughtful or caring. I tried meeting potential romances through the personal ads in the local, trendy newspaper, and found more disappointment. What was I doing wrong?

Even though love would seem to be the greatest, most easily available treasure of all, why was it so elusive? I knew I was not the only person in the world confused by love. Many people give and give as much as they can, expecting love in return, and are heartbroken when it doesn't come. I was no exception.

After many heartaches and heartbreaks, I knew I had to make a dramatic shift in the way I was looking at life. Instead of expecting love to come to me, I had to open up to the love that was already there! I had to wake up to a new way of looking at life, to find a way to be filled with love all by myself. In this process I realized my search for love was really my search for divine love—the higher, unconditional love of God that is within us and all around us in different forms and experiences. Had I found a way to tap divine love first, I would not have needed to search at all. Perhaps I can save you some wear and tear on your journey to love.

DOES GOD REALLY LOVE ME?

We've all heard the words "God loves you," perhaps since childhood, but how many of us have believed them? Some of us have even had a spiritual education that included the concept of God as Love and ourselves as expressions of that Love. Therefore, we have an unlimited supply of love within us and around us, we've been told. I may have believed it mentally, but certainly not in my heart or subconscious mind. My self-esteem was so low I didn't really believe anyone loved me at all.

Finding small ways to experience love in my life, I gradually pulled myself out of the muck I was in, toward a much brighter, happier existence.

It was a slow process of experimentation for me, but I hope to make your journey easier, more fruitful, and faster. The techniques I share are the very ones I discovered through sheer necessity. They're the means I used to drive out the horrible pain in my heart when I was alone, feeling rejected and abandoned. These methods filled that same heart with unconditional, divine love, helping me get exactly what I wanted: instant love, comfort, and security.

As much as I wanted someone to love me, I had to face an important fact—the only way for others to love me was for *me* to love myself. To do this, I had to accept the greatest, most unconditional love of all—the higher love of God (or whatever higher power you believe in). In other words, I had to "think myself loved."

After a good, long while of practicing this, I finally began to believe that love is within me and surrounds me always and that I truly am loved. I found much more happiness by myself, even though I still wanted a husband.

It became less important to have *any*one and more important to wait for *someone special*, someone who reflected God's love for me. I decided that I was finished dating and that *he* would have to find *me*—and guess what?

He showed up, just when I had given up and decided single life wasn't so bad, after all. My husband is all I ever dreamed of in spiritual, mental, emotional, and physical harmony and more—he even cooks! But no, he's not perfect, and neither am I.

DOES A RELATIONSHIP OR MARRIAGE GUARANTEE LOVE?

Even in marriage, I must always remember that it's up to me to *feel* loved and to fill myself with love. I am still learning to receive all my husband wants to give me, as well as the divine love that exists in life all around me.

Marriage can be a wonderful source of affection and solace, friendship, and companionship. Yet it's not the ultimate source of love. Single people can feel just as much love, if not more! How many people do you know who feel *constantly* loved in a marriage? One person may be cranky or depressed, out of sorts, out of town, or simply "out to lunch." What if one person needs affection and the other just needs space?

Life is not so perfect that other people, even spouses, can give us what we need all the time (or even part of the time, in some cases). You can always get what you need, however.

What if your marriage is great? There is still no guarantee you will be together forever. In fact, there's every chance you won't, since *everything* in this world is only temporary, of course. Death is a natural part of life. What do we do if our partner dies? Grieve the loss and go on with life, and hope there's enough love in the world to fill that awful void. There *is* enough love. In fact, there is an endless supply of God's love, just waiting for us to accept it.

Most people think that love equals romance and that the only way to get love is from another person. That type of love is wonderful and sweet, yet it can turn to something else very quickly, especially when one is too needy.

We will explore how to tap a much more satisfying and permanent source of love than emotional love. Does that sound impossible? It's not. This higher love is very real and much more fulfilling than any love you can imagine. Once you experience it, you will be more satisfied in any of your relationships, because no matter what happens, you will be filled with divine love. Also, relationships improve tremendously when both people are giving and receiving a higher kind of love.

As many of us sadly know, just having a relationship is not proof positive of having a life filled with love. The proof is in how you feel about yourself and your life, and mostly how you feel inside. When you feel full of love just by breathing in the sounds, smells, and experiences of life, you will know that you have learned to "think yourself loved."

LIVING IN A STATE OF DIVINE LOVE

It really doesn't matter who or what we are looking for; we will always find only one thing in the end—ourselves. Other people only reflect who we are and how we treat ourselves and others. In them we see our own fears and low self-worth or our own loving attitudes. Looking in a mirror can be very scary, but since everyone we look at mirrors us, we may as well begin to look into ourselves directly. This way we can find and bring out the good and noble qualities of true Self, the divine being we really, truly are now and will be throughout eternity.

Something You Can Do NOW:

1. Look into a mirror and pretend you are someone else looking at you. Imagine you're a higher being, your guardian angel or your spiritual teacher, looking into your eyes. Imagine how this being might see you when looking at you with love. The being may look deep into your eyes and see the spark of life that you are as soul.

2. Say, "I love you, (your name here)." Do this every time you look into a mirror, whether silently or out loud. Notice how you feel in the days to come.

3. To take this one step beyond, you may try imagining the voice of God saying to you, "I love you, (your name here)." Notice how this makes you feel. Do you doubt God's love for you? Do this for one week as an exercise in divine love. See how it makes you feel about yourself and others. Note your findings in your journal.

❤ ❤ ❤

When you are able to love yourself on a spiritual level, loving your higher Self, then you are also loving all life and loving God. Who are you but a part of life, and therefore a part of God's creation? What greater way of serving the Greatest Love of All, than by loving the part of Creation that you are? In doing so, you will be able to relax with life, knowing that you are here because you belong here and because you are loved.

I know and feel with all my heart that the true Self's natural state is love. When I am in this natural state, somehow everything and everyone seem to be in the proper place. Life appears in divine order and I am at peace with the world.

What exactly *is* divine love?

Unity cofounder Charles Fillmore explains in *The Revealing Word*: "Love is an inner quality that sees good everywhere and in everybody. It insists that all is good, and by refusing to see anything but good it causes that quality finally to appear uppermost in itself, and in all things" (p. 125).

Love, he further notes, is "the pure essence of Being that binds together the whole human family" (p. 124). In other words, love is a powerful superglue that holds all creation together. It is a consciousness that literally patches up appearances of brokenness and brings harmony, happiness, and freedom to our lives.

When I allow fear, anxiety, anger, or resentment to get in love's way, then I see the world as a hostile place, with no help in sight. Here's what *I* do, and you may want to try it too:

Something You Can Do:

1. When negative emotion tries to get in the way of love, simply turn it all over to God saying, "Bless this in the name of God" or "Bless this situation with divine love." Then say, "Thy will be done." Imagine you will be in a state of divine love and inner peace within five minutes. Imagination is your divine gift and is very powerful when used for love.

2. Do your best to let go of any fear about the situation. There is a wonderful book titled *The Secret of Letting Go* by Guy Finley that taught me to simply say, "I don't know what to do" and remain open to inner guidance and ideas from life. Try this also if you feel especially attached to your emotions. Listening (and relistening) to the audio program *Let Go, Let God* by Wally Amos will help reinforce your commitment to let go.

3. Some negative emotions can stem from physical-health issues. Love yourself enough to spend the time and money you would on your car, your child, or your loved one. See a doctor to be sure you do not have a food allergy, chemical imbalance, or hormonal imbalance that may cause mood swings or overreactions to life's challenges. There are many natural ways to combat these difficulties, such as homeopathy, Chinese medicine, and nutritional counseling. If the natural methods do not work for you or feel comfortable to you, see a medical doctor. Your emotional health and well-being are as important as your physical health.

RECOGNIZING AND APPRECIATING
GOD'S LOVE

God's love may not be what you expect it to be. For years I expected it to feel like human love and to be soft and gentle. Sometimes life hands us a challenge we feel will crush us. This, too, is God's love, strengthening us for the day when we need to keep our hearts open with compassion for our fellow souls. Sometimes this love feels very freeing, light, and airy. I feel loved for just who I am at this very moment, and I know that all is well in my world. When I look for this great, undying, unconditional love, I find it in the most unexpected places—a bird's song, a perfect flower, a call from a friend, the rain, even a great meal!

It can be a discipline to look for love, but a discipline very worthwhile. I feel blessed and grateful for the love I find when I remember to look for it. Try actually *looking* for love when you feel there's not enough love in your life. The following exercise may help you expand your capacity to see and feel love all around you.

Something You Can Do NOW:

1. Think of all the people, pets, children, relatives, coworkers, friends, schoolmates, and churchmates, who have ever loved you. Think of the love they have had or will have for you, no matter what amount of love it may seem to you. Gather all the love you feel from them in your heart.

2. Now give it all to God (or to whatever you call the higher power in your life).

3. Rest in this moment and see what you get back!

❤ ❤ ❤

The desire for a loving relationship (aside from human need for love and affection) on a higher level is really about the desire for a loving relationship with God, or your higher Self. When you open up to divine love and find a way to tap it directly, the desire for a mate comes into balance.

How does one tap this divine love? By imagining or envisioning it!

I learned to experience whatever I wanted in life by imagining it first in my mind. I would practice feeling, hearing, seeing, tasting, and touching the experience as if it were already happening, right now. Try this for yourself, being bold and unafraid. Once I experienced what I wanted to in my mind, it became my reality, sooner or later.

I applied this same principle to bringing love into my life, and it always worked. Eventually I learned to create the feeling of divine love, so that the love I attracted was a higher love.

Living in the state of this divine love got me to the point where I was no longer obsessed about looking for love. I could relax and enjoy my life, knowing that the pure, unconditional love surrounding me would attract just the right person to me. As a matter of fact, it attracted someone who also lives in this divine love most of the time.

That was what I truly wanted, a mate who also understood that there's a love far beyond what our human selves could share. We are able to understand when one of us is more centered in that love and feeling very introspective. We then have the freedom to move forward spiritually, each in his or her own way.

BEYOND LOVING YOURSELF IS ACCEPTING DIVINE LOVE

For years I worked on loving myself in obvious ways such as giving myself gifts or taking time for myself; I thought that was all I could do. I was looking for love in my life and finding it in simple things, but I was still unhappy. I was still lonely and afraid that I would not find the love I needed. Then one day I realized I was still limiting myself. I could go beyond this level of loving myself by opening myself more to God's love. In doing so, I found a much greater, higher level of loving myself.

In order to fully accept love from myself or from anyone else, I had to accept God's love as the primary source of love in all. This was the magic that took me beyond my limits to love. Once I began to tap into this pure, unconditional love, I noticed it was easier and easier to take good care of myself, to treat myself well. It became second nature to live life with more joy. Living a life filled with divine love is my greatest gift to God, to all life. The rest of this book will show you how you can do this too.

If you contemplate the stories in this book which speak to your heart and use the exercises which jump out at you, you will find yourself well on the way to the greatest freedom you have ever known—the freedom to love and be loved, whether alone or in a crowd, whether married or single. How badly do you want this freedom? The small effort you put forth to give yourself love will pay off a thousand times over. It has for me, and I certainly know it will for you too. Read on for the varied ways to do this.

CHAPTER 2

Why Loving Yourself Gets You More Love

"YOU CAN'T GIVE FROM AN EMPTY BUCKET," a wise woman once told me. That pearl of wisdom changed my life. It hit me like a ton of bricks that I had been trying for years to give without receiving, to give without filling my own love bucket, as so many of us compulsive givers do.

Once I realized I had been doing all the giving, refusing to receive, I turned that around. It took quite some time, but the results were dramatic.

I found out that I could *think myself loved*. Filling myself with love only helped me give more love to others, and *get* more as well. I felt full of love, literally, and overflowing with love to give. When I finally gave from a full heart, there was a bonus: I became much more attractive to others.

Why?

What happens when you give a greater amount of unconditional love? When you glow with love, how do people treat you? When you are happy and fulfilled, do you notice how heads turn and sparkling eyes meet yours with warmth and love in return?

When you are filled with love, when you love yourself, when you *think* you are loved, others love you too! Now you have *double* the love—the love you give yourself and the love others give you because you have become an attractive force for their love, like metal to a magnet.

Throughout this book you will have the opportunity to try dozens of ways to fill yourself with this love, and I encourage you to try the ones that "sing" to you. Listen for their song.

Before you practice loving yourself, you might want to be sure you feel okay about it. We are so often raised to believe that everyone else is more important than we are, that everyone else is more deserving of love, and that it is an ego trip to love ourselves.

Is It an Ego Trip to Love Yourself?

I used to think it was self-centered to love myself, and I know that many of us have been taught this. However, over the years I've noticed that people filled with love for themselves and for others are rarely on an ego trip and that they give more love unconditionally. Notice how this works by paying attention to the opposite type, the person with the biggest ego in your life.

An ex-boss of mine had such little self-esteem that

she was constantly putting other people down if they were slimmer, smarter, or more attractive than she was. She was completely unaware of the anger she carried. Literally frightening people away, she kept out any sort of threat to her extremely weak sense of her true Self. She was unable to recognize her own real beauty and inner strength, so she had to use outer "force" to experience her self-worth.

My own feelings of inadequacy have at times caused me to want to feel better or smarter than others, a fairly common aspect of human nature. It's why we secretly feel a little bit better when we find out someone else has goofed—especially if it's a serious goof! We know then that we are, no doubt, superior (ahem!). It is the mind's way of comparing and compiling data to see how we are doing in life. We all like to give *ourselves* gold stars, of course.

Now think about people you know who are centered and self-confident and who seem to love themselves. They surround themselves with loving people, beautiful surroundings, enjoyable work. Notice that they have no need to criticize others, find fault, or gossip. They love and understand others because they love and understand themselves.

The healthiest, most balanced egos belong to the people who love themselves and have little need to put others down or trumpet their own success. The most inflated, disproportionate egos belong to the people who feel the least secure, needing to act big and obvious in order to be noticed, like a hot-air balloon! People who need to "toot their own horn" in order to feel acknowledged have yet to learn how to acknowledge themselves on a deeper, more substantial level.

So, does loving yourself mean you will develop a big ego? Explore the answer for yourself in this writing exercise.

Note: You may want to begin a special journal based upon your adventure into loving yourself and use it to do the writing exercises throughout the book.

Something You Can Do NOW:

1. Think about how you'd feel if you truly loved everything about yourself and your life. How do you think you would treat others? Would you be ordering people about, expecting to be catered to? Would you feel the need to spread bad news or to gossip? Would you feel that you were more important than others or (more likely) would you treat others kindly and with patience, love, and caring?

2. Imagine how wonderful it would feel to be in love with life. Write the way you feel, as if it's happening right now.

3. Now, ask yourself whether you feel self-centered or generous and giving.

LOVING YOURSELF CREATES A WAY TO GIVE MORE LOVE TO OTHERS

From loving myself more, I feel more in love with life and I have more to give. When I feel filled to the brim, love can pour out easily to those around me. This love that flows out of me leaves room for more love to come in. As

I give more love out, I feel even more coming in, because now I've expanded my capacity for love, both in giving and receiving.

When I give to myself, I have less need for others to give to me. It doesn't mean I don't need other people; of course I do! But when I'm feeling really lonely, now I know how to rest in the arms of love. I can drink in the love that is life itself, which we are constantly given from our divine source, or higher power.

TO FEEL AND GIVE MORE LOVE, IMAGINE YOU'RE IN LOVE!

Think about how you feel when you're in love. When you're in love, just newly matched with someone, do you feel that everyone around you deserves love? Do you treat people as if they were royalty? Do you love even the gray, rainy days? If you're like me, when you're in love, you don't care if you have to wait in traffic. You feel good just to be alive. Imagine feeling that way *all the time*. How much more loving might you be toward yourself and toward others? Try the following exercise for a sense of this wonderful feeling.

Something You Can Do NOW:

Imagine this as clearly as you can, using all of your senses: Your very own Prince/Princess Charming rides up to you on a magnificent white horse. She/he is dressed in much finery and is obviously feeling very comfortable.

Looking fit and healthy, she/he is relaxed and calm. A quiet self-confidence exudes from every pore.

She/he is emotionally stable and balanced, feeling and expressing all that is within his/her heart—kindness; pure, unconditional love; and truth. She/he has no hidden anger or fear, only love. She/he knows exactly what she/he wants and is willing to do anything ethical and loving to obtain it. There's a very open heart residing within him/her and it speaks of a love so rare that it can only come from one place—heaven itself.

Let this feeling of love surround you and linger as you go about your day.

There's no harm in imagining yourself surrounded by love, as long as you don't expect it from any particular source. In fact, not trying to control or limit where it comes from can only bring more love to you. And here's a secret—look for love in the smallest, most unlikely places, including a smile from a stranger or an unexpected gift from a child. These can be so uplifting that they make your whole day brighter!

WOULDN'T IT BE WONDERFUL TO MEET SOMEONE LIKE YOUR IMAGINARY PRINCE OR PRINCESS?

Isn't it what we all want for ourselves, and isn't it what we all want to be? We can find people with some of these traits, but rarely, if ever, all of them.

Ask yourself: Do *I* possess the qualities I am looking for in a mate or companion? Would I fall in love with me, as I am, based on my kindness, compassion, honesty, sense of humor, and so on? The secret is that the more we develop the traits for which we are looking, the more we attract others with these same traits. An even deeper secret is that the more we treat ourselves with kindness, truth, unconditional love, and acceptance, the more others treat us with these qualities. People treat us exactly as we treat ourselves.

I, like many other people, have had narrow escapes from detrimental relationships of one kind or another. At one period in my life I attracted men who were very dishonest with me. Why was this happening to me? I wondered whether I was just too trusting or too gullible.

Finally one day in a flash of realization, I saw that I had been less than honest with myself (who, me?). If I'd thought about what I was *really* feeling, I would not have stayed in the relationship as long as I did. I would have been willing to recognize the difficulties much earlier. Now I try to be as honest as I can with myself about what I really, truly want and need.

It works!

Most of the men I dated before I was married were good people; they were just emotionally immature, as was I. They reflected weaknesses of my own with which I wasn't yet ready to deal.

One of those weaknesses was that I didn't give myself enough time. I was attracting men who spent very little time with me. I couldn't understand why this kept happening. I began to get some insight as I looked at my life and saw the truth: *I spent very little time with myself.* I had not been enjoying life, watching the sunset, cooking myself a nice meal, reading a good book, or just *being*. I was working almost constantly—whether it was my job, my volunteer work, or some project around the house.

Even though I had no children to care for as so many people I know do (how on earth do you do it?), I still found a zillion ways to keep myself busy. By keeping a journal and asking God for guidance, I later realized something very important: Keeping busy was just my subconscious way of avoiding the emotional pain of my past. I knew I had to face that pain sooner or later. If I wanted peace and love in my life, it had to be now.

So I started spending more time with myself, and guess what? You got it—the men I attracted were spending more time with me.

Could I attract a man who could make a commitment yet? No way. Had I made any commitments to myself? No, I really hadn't.

Once I began making and keeping promises to myself, things improved even more. There will be more in later chapters on how to pinpoint your reflection in disappointing relationships and what to do about it. For now, just try to be the observer, like a good reporter who watches everything with a nonjudgmental view. You know, "Just the facts, ma'am."

IS IT SELFISH TO LOVE YOURSELF?

I often used to think that the term *loving yourself* implied a great degree of self-centered narcissism, thinking of no one else and being quite rude and uncaring. However, *not* loving myself certainly didn't seem to help *anyone*. I decided to try loving myself instead and discovered that by doing so, I had much more love to give others. What could be selfish about that?

How does the dictionary define *selfish*? My dictionary (*American Heritage*, Houghton Mifflin, 1969) defines it as: "concerned chiefly or only with oneself, *without regard* [my emphasis] for the well-being of others." When you truly love yourself, are you disregarding others?

In my own experience and in observing the experiences of many others, I have seen how much loving yourself helps other people and is in fact the only way to actually give to others in a truly heartfelt, unconditional manner. Then you expect nothing in return, because you don't need it! You've already given what you need to yourself or, at the very least, simply asked someone to give it to you.

Giving from an empty bucket is impossible. So, if *not* loving yourself means you have less to give others (empty bucket), doesn't loving yourself (filling your bucket so you have more to give others) seem like the *least* selfish, most generous thing to do? In my humble opinion, others have a greater regard and respect for you when you can give to them out of fullness, out of a desire to give rather than a need to receive. I know this because I tried to give for so long with expectations of return. I had a rude awakening. People could only give back to me as much as I could give to myself, and only when I gave to them unconditionally.

WHY DO PEOPLE WHO GIVE SO MUCH LOVE TO OTHERS GET SO LITTLE LOVE THEMSELVES?

Is it because they're unlovable? Hardly! They're usually the most cuddly, lovable people you could ever hope to meet. They often face one simple, but not easy, challenge: loving themselves enough to let true love into their lives. Here's one of the simple visualization exercises I used to help me love myself and open myself to the purest, most secure and satisfying love there is.

Something You Can Do NOW:

Visualize yourself as an open vessel, such as a beautiful vase of flowers, ready to receive the water that your caretaker pours upon you. Imagine this water is pure, unconditional divine love flowing from its source down to you. Feel it filling you with the most incredible sense of being refreshed, adored, and cared-for greatly.

Carry this feeling with you into your next task, as you fall asleep each night, and as you awaken each day.

❤ ❤ ❤

I invite you to make up your own exercise—one that suits your own spiritual beliefs and lifestyle. If you do this sort of thing daily, I guarantee you will be graced with much more love in your life.

My own life has improved so much with my new ability to receive love that I am awestruck when I look back. It was not always so easy, and I hope the long and arduous journey I took will make yours much easier through the stories and exercises still to come.

CHAPTER 3

The Way I Learned to Love Myself

DESPERATION IS THE REAL MOTHER OF INVENTION.
That's how I learned to love myself—through desperation.

Imagine a beautiful island paradise—turquoise water, warm sun, white beaches with palm trees to cool you. Imagine breathtaking pink-and-orange sunsets and the scent of tropical flowers on the breeze. Imagine perfect air, the kind that caresses you as you gracefully glide through it toward . . . what?

When I lived in Hawaii, I felt as if I were truly in paradise, but the loneliest kind of paradise I could imagine— no dear friends, no intimate relationship. I had wanted to go to Hawaii, so I imagined being there. I did so well that I even ended up living there. But I was still lonely, even in such a magnificent place. How did I get to this point in my life? And how did I get past it to greater happiness?

25

It all started when I was born, believe it or not. My biological mother was in a deep depression—so deep that she couldn't take care of her children properly. The basics, like food and love, were not available to her children when needed, and of course, love is as essential as food to an infant.

I was definitely not held and loved enough, if at all, and likely not fed enough. Good thing I'm by nature a survivor! My sister remembers that I lay in my crib and cried a lot. By the time I was three months old, my mother was placed in a mental institution. The institution advised my father to divorce her, since they had diagnosed her as schizophrenic and held little hope of recovery.

I never saw my mother again. When she was in her 60's, she died alone in her apartment in New York. No one knew for days, I heard. Would I end up like her?

After my mother was gone, my father had his own psychological problems and pain to deal with, and four of us children to raise by himself. He had trouble finding steady work. None of the relatives, except my aging grandparents, were willing to care for us.

My father's parents *did* take us in. While we were, no doubt, a handful, they were both very angry people, expressing their anger with physical force and a belt every so often. Such treatment isn't very encouraging to anyone's self-esteem, especially that of small children. Also, we were quite poor, so food wasn't abundant there either. Feeling insecure became more and more natural to me.

Within a few years, it was time to give my father's parents a rest. My father brought us to Colorado to be placed in foster homes, because he now had a job as a postal worker there.

As you can see, up to this time I hadn't experienced even a semisecure form of love. Now, at the still delicate age of six years, I would lose not only my grandparents, the only consistent adult presence in my life so far, but also my sisters and brothers, the only true family I had known. I was to be completely without anyone or anything familiar.

After placing us in foster homes, my father said he would find us a home and mother so we would be a family again. He couldn't live up to that promise. He found a woman to marry, but she didn't want to be burdened with children, so he put us up for adoption.

Even though I had not been able to count on my father up to then, I still innocently worshipped him. Later in life, I transferred this hero worship to men who I hoped would be my saviors in love, even when they were obviously no longer interested, available, or committed.

After one failed foster home, I was adopted at age seven by a very caring couple. However, like many people of their generation, it was difficult for them to express that caring in words or touch. They both had experienced very difficult, love-deficient childhoods themselves. I withdrew from loving or trusting any immediate family members.

At a very early age, I turned to friends outside my family. I felt as though I were alone in all the world. I longed for a boyfriend who would love me and take me away from my pain, from my loneliness. This began as early as the first grade! To this day, I remember a boy named Glenn. He had to move away, so I kissed him good-bye on the cheek (our first and last kiss). He was another male in my life to leave and never return. This pattern was to repeat itself many times, far into my adult life.

As I matured (if you can call it that!) I found lots of boyfriends along the way—and even a husband, for a very brief time. Still, the loneliness remained. None of my romantic relationships, including my first marriage, lasted more than two years; most lasted less than six months. Even platonic friendships did not seem to deepen.

The men I attracted were unable to make a commitment to *me* but would often marry the very next woman they dated! It took me years to get a clue. They had obviously been *able* to commit. What I hadn't been seeing was that *I* was the one who had the problem, not the men I dated! Looking back, I see that even many of my friendships were social friendships, rather than true bonds of love and caring.

That came clearly to light during one painful time. Something happened to drive home the point that I had become very lonely and isolated. After a dog bit me on the foot, I could barely walk and had to crawl to the bathroom the first night after the bite. I tried to think of someone I could call to help me. I couldn't think of anyone.

I'd already told some of my friends about the injury, and no one had offered assistance. I, of course, didn't feel worthy enough to *ask*. Looking back now, I feel sure they would have helped had they known I wanted them to.

What made me really sad was becoming acutely aware of the fact that I didn't feel I had even one true-blue friend—someone who would be there if I needed her.

WHAT WAS I DOING WRONG?

I was blaming the friends or my choice of friendships. It wasn't until my mid-thirties that I began to realize that *they* were not to blame, but *I was*.

When I was growing up, my family did the best they could to express love in many ways. I was the one who withdrew when my adoptive mother tried to hug me. She gave up after a couple of tries, because she had her own insecurities.

I was resistant to love. If someone had truly been my friend, I wouldn't have been able to maintain the friendship for long. It was not part of my repertoire. I simply did not know how to receive love.

Once I realized the problem, I called a friend who was just about as frustrated as I was and we brainstormed for four hours about how to love ourselves more. I'll never forget that day, because it was New Year's Day, 1983, a new beginning (probably the most important day of my life in many ways). It was also the longest phone conversation of my life!

We both understood the idea of being responsible for our feelings and choices. We also knew there are often deep-seated, unconscious psychological patterns that affect those choices.

My friend and I explored some possible reasons and

solutions. We came up with one that stood out above all else: We both needed to *love ourselves more.* The only question now was, *How?*

We thought of a few simple beginnings, such as buying ourselves fresh flowers and saying "no" when it was the truest answer of our hearts. We talked about the things we did for others and wondered why we did only a fraction of those kindnesses for ourselves.

HOW COULD I LEARN TO LOVE MYSELF MORE?

After that painfully honest and in-depth dialogue, I resolved to begin immediately doing as many nice things for myself as I could think of. I was surprised beyond belief at how *difficult* and challenging it was to do simple things for myself with love. For example, I decided I would buy fresh flowers for myself weekly, no matter what got in the way. There was a fresh-flower stand just a mile from my home. I would get a wonderful bouquet of fresh flowers in season just by putting a single dollar in a box.

What a refreshing, delightful feeling it was to buy something special for myself! Unfortunately, I felt a twinge of guilt every time I spent seemingly unnecessary money on myself—and all for just a single greenback!

It still amazes me what a tremendous effort it was then (and still is, at times) to be generous or even courteous to *myself.* It was okay, even desirable, for me to give to others, expecting of course that they would give in return. Yet there was still a big part of me that was not open or ready to receive love or gifts from others. If I did receive from others, I felt obligated to immediately give something back. Sound familiar?

The magical thing about buying myself flowers—or *anything*, it seemed—was that other people actually started buying them for me too! If I forgot or couldn't find time to get fresh flowers that week, someone I knew would bring me some! The flowers became a symbol for me of how much more I was loving myself. They were proof that I was now taking responsibility for making myself happy, rather than waiting and hoping that someone else would.

How could someone else read my mind and give me exactly what I needed, just exactly when I needed it? A sun began to rise inside me and light up a whole new world. It dawned on me that I was truly the only one who could make myself happy. With this realization I took back the power to create a happy life—the power I'd been giving to everyone except myself.

Something You Can Do NOW:

1. Think of a gift you've been wanting for your birthday or a holiday. This can be something you've hoped someone would notice that you want or need.

    Write the gift in your journal or here: _____

    _____.

2. Make a commitment RIGHT NOW to get this gift for yourself. Sign and date this like a contract in your

journal or right here: _____
_____ date_____.
If you don't have the money right now, you can:

Save $2 a week in a specially marked envelope.

Go to a secondhand store or thrift shop and look for the item.

Do some extra work or think about what you might sell to get it.

Imagine you're buying it now (and your action will follow your thought).

I BUILT A ROAD INTO MY HEART THAT OTHERS COULD TRAVEL

As I began doing nice little things for myself, I started seeing an image of two roads. One road went into my heart and one went out. The outgoing road was a six-lane superhighway, smoothly paved and kept in top-notch condition. The pavement always looked brand-new. I thought of it as an out-giving road. That was the road I had built by giving to others. The incoming (receiving) one was a little country road—unpaved and full of rocks and potholes and having broken-down barbed-wire fences strewn everywhere. How could anyone possibly get in?

Obviously, I had not kept the incoming road in good repair. However, I was beginning to see that the only way anyone could give to me, could travel that road in, was for me to repair it and smooth it *by giving to myself*. I knew that was the only way.

If you like, you can use this image for yourself. Every

time you do something nice for yourself, imagine you're paving the "road in" just a little more. For most of us, it is truly the road less traveled.

The next step for me after giving myself flowers was to begin getting massages regularly. This was extravagant for my budget, but I found a way to do it. Massage students need people on whom to practice, and—lucky for me—my neighbor was studying massage.

You can try calling a massage school if you want to use this idea. There is little or no charge for this service with students. Or, if you prefer, you can just take a nice hot bath once a week as a loving-yourself ritual. Light candles and put some special mineral salts in the bath for fuller relaxation. Give a massage to your feet, scalp, face, hands, arms, and legs. See how great it feels to be that caring and gentle with yourself.

Enjoying sunsets by myself became a new goal. Prior to loving myself, I had always felt the need for someone special with whom to share the beauty of nature. It was as though I wasn't worthy of enjoying the magnificence of life all by myself.

After a while I realized that I really could have anything I wanted. I didn't have to wait for someone else to help me enjoy it, as though I wasn't worthy of it alone. For instance, I'd been waiting to think about buying new furniture until I got married again. Years went by and the prospects weren't great. One day something inside me clicked, and I realized I had been waiting for someone to enjoy the new furniture with—someone worthy or someone who would "make me whole" by being my "other half." As soon as I realized what I was doing to my self-image, I set a goal to refurbish my entire home, and did so within a year.

The next big step was a new car. I'd always wanted a snazzy car, and since I was in sales, I *needed* something that looked nice. I had thought about this for years, but thought I couldn't afford it. I realized that I was limiting myself and that I could somehow find a way. I decided to take the plunge and lease the car of my dreams. The night I took the car home I couldn't sleep. Some insecure part of me inside said: "You don't deserve a car this nice. You aren't worthy of a car this nice!" Shaking inside, I was ready to take the car back as soon as the sun came up and the dealership opened. Somehow I forced myself to get up and make a cup of tea. When times are hard, hot tea can be a great comforter. It always seemed to make me feel more secure.

The tea worked its magic, and I was back on track. "Debbie," I told myself, "you are going to keep that car if I have to force you!" And I *did* have to force myself to keep it! However, within one or two days, I began to actually feel comfortable with it, and in turn, with the "new me." That car will always be a powerful symbol for me of how I gained a new level of self-esteem.

Now, I know it may seem more like narcissistic love for me to have given myself all these gifts. It was simply my way of accepting myself as no better or worse than anyone else, but equally as deserving. Realizing that it was okay to be happy, okay to accept God's gifts of earth as of heaven, I was free. Or at least I *thought* I was!

There was one more gift I had to give myself before I could open up to a more direct flow of God's love anytime I wanted it.

I'd always dreamed of taking myself on a cruise. Okay, I admit it. I was a *Love Boat* fanatic. Of course, I have always been magnetically drawn to anything having to do with love! That's what happens when you get too little of it. I had also dreamed of visiting Hawaii. After earning more money (resulting from the effect of my newly found self-esteem), I combined both dreams and went on a cruise in paradise, around the Hawaiian Islands.

After that beautiful but very lonely cruise, I moved to Hawaii because it called to me. In many ways, I did feel as if I were in paradise. I could watch the boat races at sunset from the window of my high-rise condo in Makiki. I could see the beach at Waikiki from my cozy twenty-fifth floor apartment. I was in the most beautiful place I had ever been. I had much to make me happy, but I wasn't. Something was *still* missing, after all I had given myself.

I looked for that missing ingredient in potential romance, but I couldn't attract anyone I would even care to consider. This was unusual for me. In the past, I had had no trouble attracting men whom I thought worthwhile. *Keeping* them was the problem!

I was like a wanderer in a desert, thirsty for a drop of water, with an oasis right in front of me. But I didn't feel worthy to drink of the water.

I was being forced to look within for love.

Finally, desperation took over and I discovered a way to reach the truest, most direct source of love that exists.

I went into that oasis and drank from the purest fountain there is, the fountain of God, Life, or whatever you choose to call this higher power whose love for us exceeds all bounds. The feeling of being totally, unconditionally loved simply for being a spark of God, and being *me*, brought tears to my eyes.

Here's how I did it: I imagined love in the best way I could. I thought of it as a fountain, flowing for me, all day and all night. I made up a little exercise to feel this love whenever I felt lonely and unloved.

There is an oasis in front of us all constantly; yet how can we find it? And if we find it, how can we feel worthy to drink of its eternal fountain of love?

Perhaps your answer will be to enjoy more fully the simple things in life, such as a sunset, a walk by the ocean, or even the use of your divine gift of imagination, like I did. You may want to practice this right now.

Something You Can Do NOW:

Sit quietly and take a few deep breaths. Each time you breathe out, release any stress by imagining all the tension in your body flowing out, along with your out-breath.

Imagine you are walking through a vast, lonely desert. You can feel the sand shifting under your feet as the sun's warmth penetrates your clothing. The only sound is the wind, which adds to your throat's dry, parched feeling. You feel as though you're the only soul for miles upon miles. A green speck appears in front of you. It could be an oasis. You become hopeful and continue to move in the direction of the bright green area in the distance. You get close enough to see that it *is* an oasis. As you get much closer to it, you hear the most beautiful melody on earth coming from its center.

Now imagine yourself walking into this oasis. You are struck by the beauty of the lovely white-marble fountain in its center. Next to the fountain stands your guardian angel. Filled with love and the light of heaven, she/he offers you a golden cup filled with liquid from this fountain. You accept it gratefully. The water is sweet and pure, more refreshing than anything you've ever drunk. You feel its magical quality filling you with the most sublime, unconditional love you've ever felt. She/he then invites you to step into the fountain. You do so and feel completely surrounded by this love.

Know here and now that this is God's love for you. This feeling can be gotten directly at any moment simply by opening your heart to being filled with it and allowing it to encompass you like a warm hug. Imagine this is happening now.

How did that feel?

Perhaps you can think of this love like a puppy just waiting for a signal to jump into your lap. This love is waiting for you constantly. Love exists always, and you are allowed to feel it anytime you wish!

When I was in the process of learning how to love myself more, I realized that Spirit was very patiently waiting to shower me with its love. It doesn't give more than one asks for or can receive. I still have to work on accepting more love, but what more joyful work could there be?

Once I had some idea of how to go about loving myself in the ultimate manner—receiving God's love—giving myself gifts of time, enjoyment of some material things in life, and appreciation of nature became the ways I learned to accept God's love in my life.

All I had to do next was continue to do these things and notice when it became difficult for me to give myself love. I had to become aware of any blocks that got in the way of giving to myself and receiving more love.

DID I HAVE IT ALL TOGETHER YET? YOU BE THE JUDGE

My thermostat for detecting blocks to receiving love came into play when I felt unhappy. If things weren't going my way and I got frustrated, angry, hurt, or sad, I stopped and took a good look. Even though I had been doing all these wonderful things for myself, I still had a pain in my heart that it seemed would not heal.

I thought I was pretty good at loving myself, and I *was*, partially. I just hadn't found a way to be without this old emotional pain. That's when I decided I needed to get really creative. I made up an exercise for myself and used it every single day when I finished working. I usually lay down on my bed, relaxed, and allowed myself to fall asleep if I felt like it.

This exercise engages the imagination, our divine gift, to open our hearts to the healing love of the highest within us and the divine love that is ours, if we're open to receiving it. You can try this exercise too!

Something You Can Do:

1. Every day after work or before sleeping, breathe deeply a few times and relax. Pay attention to the sound of your breathing. This will relax you. Now think of where you feel emotional pain in your body. Is it in your chest? Your stomach? Your head? Wherever it is, imagine filling that area with blue light, which is calming and healing for the emotions.

   In addition, you can use a holy word that is dear to you or the sound of HU, an ancient love song to God. Pronounced like the word *hue*, it is sung in a long, drawn-out breath (*Huuuuuuuu*) repeatedly for a few minutes. HU can be found in many different cultures and religions. The word *hallelujah* was derived from the sound of HU, and can be heard in sounds of life all around us. If you prefer, sing "Hallelujah" or any spiritual phrase that you feel is powerful and comforting for you. You can speak or sing silently to yourself or out loud, or just imagine beautiful, uplifting music.

2. As you fill this area of pain within you with light and sound, add love to it. Feel the love you have for the little child you were who got hurt. Feel God's love for you healing the old wounds.

   WHAT TO EXPECT: If you do this exercise regularly, you may be surprised by some of the wonderful consequences. But first, you may feel some emotions needing to be cleansed. Emotions are normally felt and then released. However, if there is trauma associated with those emotions, then the emotions are suppressed until we are fully able to experience them, which is how they are released. Unfortunately, they can be released at the most embarrassing times, when we're totally unprepared. A button may be pushed inside us, but we may not realize it until it's too late and the damage has been done.

If you find yourself snapping at a friend or associate or if it seems your response to something is out of proportion to its importance, take responsibility in the moment. You might offer a graceful apology to your friend or family member for overreacting to the situation by explaining that you are working with some old patterns which are being released and by asking for their patience during this process.

Many therapists use methods to get us to feel things we don't want to feel. This can be good if it's really necessary. Then we can release those emotions safely and create more space for love. We often need help in dealing with very difficult emotions, so I encourage you to seek professional counseling if these emotions come up intensely.

SOME EASY WAYS TO GET THROUGH THE PROCESS OF RELEASING EMOTIONS

1. Keep breathing! This is the simplest, most obvious, but (believe it or not) most *important* thing to do! I find that if I breathe lovingly into the area of emotional pain in my body, I am able to allow myself to feel it more fully.

2. Try to notice what happens just before some intense emotions arise. *I* notice that I become anxious or impatient prior to an emotional release. When these particular feelings come up, I know that within twenty-four hours I will "blow," so I do something like #3 below as soon as I can, to bring the boiling emotions to the surface before the lid comes off unexpectedly.

3. Beat a pillow (if I am driving alone, I beat the seat next to me or scream with the windows rolled up); tear up a newspaper; take a dish towel and beat the kitchen sink (my cats think I've gone crazy, but it works and feels great!). I am amazed at how this brings up anger or tears. I almost always end up crying.

❤ ❤ ❤

I know some people who like to throw ice cubes at brick walls, against the outside of the house or onto a cement floor. Throw them as hard as you can, and imagine the old fears and negative feelings being released safely.

Releasing old pain, anger, fear, anxiety, and so on, is one of the very best loving things you can do for yourself, because it leaves more room for the love. You won't always have to know where the emotions came from. They may be from infancy or even prebirth. They may be from a situation you could never comprehend. Simply allow the layers to be peeled off as they need to be, while you fill yourself with light, sound, and love pushing out the fear.

Because I did the exercise above on a regular basis, I healed the pain in my heart. I formed a brand-new, wonderful relationship with my mother before she departed this world. My friendships are much more satisfying and balanced. Now I receive as much as I give.

I still have some challenges to overcome, as I'm sure I always will. That's what makes me grow, and I am very grateful for the opportunities. Mostly, my life is fulfilling and happy, with a lot of love to share. I do the best I can to fill myself with love, and I trust that life will keep getting better, and so it has!

CHAPTER 4

Giving Yourself Love

A FRIEND I'LL CALL "TERESA" said she'd been having problems making ends meet. There was always too much month left after the paycheck was spent. Bills were piling up and she barely had enough to buy groceries. She ended up having to borrow money from her parents to pay bills some months. Forget trying to do anything nice for herself! She was not happy with the situation, as you can well imagine.

Teresa decided to reread the original booklet version of this book, *How to Love Yourself So Others Can Love You More.* She started doing some nice things for herself by following a few of the Loving Yourself Exercises in the booklet. She took the risk and bought a few simple things she had really been needing and wanting. They didn't amount to a great expense, but were important things to her.

The most miraculous thing happened! As soon as she started giving more to *herself*, her financial situation improved and she was able to give more to *others*. She was able to pay her bills on time and even pay back her parents!

I thanked her for sharing this story, because it proved to me a pattern I'd discovered for myself, as related in the previous chapter. The more I gave to myself, the more I had to give to others! I noticed that if I saved money for myself, I earned more, so I had more to give. It seems truly magical, but in a way it also makes real sense. I felt better about myself, so I was able to receive more from life. Want to try this yourself?

Let's explore some more ways you can give love to yourself.

Something You Can Do:

1. Write down two or three things in your journal or on a slip of paper that you have needed or wanted for a while. The items could be as simple and inexpensive as a new hair barrette, brush, or comb—even new socks or underwear. How about new kitchen towels or a pretty soap dispenser for the bathroom? What about that picture frame you've been meaning to get to spruce up your bedroom? Your umbrella's broken and you live in Portland, Oregon? Oh, NO! Actually, that happened to me, and I bought a really nice one for two bucks at Goodwill when I was down on the dough. You can spend one dollar at a garage sale giving yourself a nice gift, if you're short on cash, as I was.

2. Choose one of the items on your list from #1 above and put it on your grocery list. If you need to go to a different store, *do it*. You can go to a nearby department store or pharmacy the same day you grocery shop.

3. Thank yourself for being kind to yourself. Go home and look at your new item and grin with glee. You have a right to enjoy everything life has to offer, no matter how simple. The more I am grateful for the little things, the more my needs are easily filled.

4. Pat yourself on the back and realize that you've helped not only yourself, but many others. You have helped the economy by improving the wealth of those with whom you do business and those with whom *they* do business and those with whom their vendors do business, ad infinitum! It also sends a signal to the people around you and gives them a model for being good to *them*selves. It humbles me to think that loving myself becomes a gift to all of life—and it comes full circle. Being selfish can be extremely self*less*.

WHAT IF YOU DON'T HAVE TIME TO DO ALL THOSE GREAT THINGS FOR YOURSELF?

Imagine yourself having time! Once you imagine something, action follows.

Loving yourself even applies to time. I find that the more time I give to myself, the more time I have. It's tricky at first, but you can try this as an experiment.

Something You Can Do NOW:

If you've been feeling rushed, pressured, stressed, and generally ready for membership in the rat race, do the unthinkable—set aside separate, special time just for yourself with absolutely *nothing* planned!

If you have an appointment calendar (if you don't, that may be one reason you are stressed!), get it out now. Set aside one whole afternoon every week or as many weeks as possible, in the month. Write in big letters "R&R." In military language, this means "Rest and Recreation." If you have not heard this term, you *definitely* need it! You can choose either rest or recreation, but make sure it is absolutely, positively *not* related to anything that sounds, tastes, smells, or feels like work.

I find the best way for me to have leisure time is to plan absolutely nothing and do whatever my little heart desires. In today's fast-paced, high-stressed world, doing nothing is an art many of us sorely need to cultivate.

You'll begin to find that not only do you have more time for yourself, you will also have more to give others as well.

Sound impossible?

Just try it and you will be amazed. Ever heard the old axiom that work expands to fill the time allotted? Well, it's true.

If your subconscious knows you only have a certain amount of time to do a task, then that's all the time it will take you to finish it. All kinds of things may try to get in the way, but if you simply stay focused on the idea that you *will* get your tasks done by a certain time, then you *will*.

If it seems that you have to give something up, you may look closer and find that you give chunks of time to things which aren't really important to you. Let those go, and you'll have the time for yourself.

WHAT ELSE CAN YOU DO FOR YOURSELF AND OTHERS?

Something You Can Do NOW:

1. Make a list in your journal of some things you'd like to do for yourself. The list can relate to anything in your life. The items on it don't have to require money. Remember, these are possibilities. You're simply writing them as an exercise to see how they could help you and others. You need not commit to anything on the list, unless you choose to do so.

Use the following list as a guide for ideas:

Money	Career
Family	Relationships
Hobbies	Clothing
Food	Education
Health	Friendships
Vacations	Fun
Adventure	Arts
Music	Entertainment
Sports	Relaxation

2. Next to the things you could possibly do for yourself, write down whom those things may help. For example:

WHAT	**WHOM IT WILL HELP**
1. Fun—	
Go to that new restaurant.	Me, restaurant employees, and owners, suppliers, food manufacturers, farmers, and so on
2. Arts—	
Take a pottery class.	Me, the art school, my art teacher, clay manufacturers, those who receive my pots, those who are inspired to take an art class

As you can see, the more you do for *yourself*, the more you automatically do for others. You can't help it! Isn't life grand?

WHAT MAKES YOU HAPPY?

Think about some of those things you'd like to do that you listed in the previous exercise. These are the things that make you the most happy. Sometimes they are the simplest, least expensive of all!

Here's one idea that costs absolutely nothing:

Consider making a date with yourself to see the sunset today or tomorrow, even if you have to sneak a peek from the window at work. Imagine it's the highest, purest love possible coming through a special window of heaven that opens once a day. It's there for you and everyone else. *You are part of* the One Spirit, Creator, God, or whatever you choose to call this universal life force and higher power that reveals itself as unconditional love.

As you watch the sun rise or set, see if you can feel the love of God for all creation, *including you*, coming through the light and beauty you are beholding. Feel that love melting through any remaining walls or blocks to love that you may have and caressing you with its eternal flow.

You are a human being with just as much right to use your own free will as anyone. So use it!

Something You Can Do NOW:

1. Make a list in your journal of the things you like to do or would like to do that make you happiest.

2. Choose one thing that you would like to do, and commit to it. Sign and date your commitment. Then watch as miracles happen to bring it about!

3. What makes you *un*happy? Make a list. How many of these things are necessary to keep in your life? Get help from a professional therapist if what makes you unhappy is taking over your world. Imagine yourself free.

4. Choose one thing that it's possible for you to change. Make a commitment to change it. Write, "This will change," and sign and date your declaration. Forget about *how* it will change; just write it, turn it over to God, and look for life to show you what to do next. Trust yourself to know. You may be smarter than you think!

Something Else You Can Do NOW:

1. Make a date with yourself to do something you like. Be sure you have decided exactly what you want to do first, such as what movie, play, or restaurant to go to.

2. Now invite someone to go with you. Be specific about what you're going to do, so your friend is clear that this is *your party*. For example, say this: "I'm going to my favorite restaurant for dinner and then to see the play *A Midsummer Night's Dream*. Would you like to join me?" If your friend says, "I'd rather go see the latest movie and get a sandwich," you can say that you would be happy to do that another time, but that this is a special outing for you and that your friend is welcome to come along if he or she would like to. If the answer is no, simply invite another friend or go on your own.

   This way, you'll get a feel for what you want, what makes you happy inside, and what feels right to you, instead of just going along with the wishes of others when you may not really want to. Of course, compromising is very important in any relationship, but not *this* time. This particular experience is just for you, and you can explain this to your friend or family member.

   When I first started loving myself more, I decided to really focus on what made me happiest in my life—career, exercise, hobbies, friends, and so on. One by one, I took inventory in each department of my life and began to weed out things that didn't feel comfortable to me. This took years, and I'm still watching to see if things feel comfortable and true.

I also tried to be as honest with myself as I could about what I really enjoyed. For example, in the exercise department, I thought about the fun things I liked to do. Why should I play racquetball just because it was in style or go to aerobics classes if I was sick of them? I decided I preferred individual exercise that I could control myself, like dancing at home, swimming, and hiking up and down hills near my house. For strength training I took up a system I could do at home when I had twenty minutes to spare. These choices also made my entire exercise program portable! Any time I travel, I can continue to be good to my body by exercising consistently. And I'm still doing what I love, just because I was able to be honest with myself about what made me happy!

I realized I would be much happier working for myself and setting my own work schedule. So, my higher Self helped me find a way to achieve my goal of being self-employed through writing and publishing.

Tell yourself that you will be more successful if you do what you love. It's true that you will, if you follow your heart and higher Self's true desire.

Another example of how to give yourself love came from a woman we'll call "Brenda" who told me the following story:

Brenda went on a date with a man to whom she felt attracted. She wasn't sure if he was the kind of person who would really be good for her. So why was she so attracted to him? She decided to find out.

When Brenda got home, she sat down and looked within herself to see where the attraction was really coming from. She discovered that she needed to be in her dad's lap, a child again, being held and cuddled and loved.

She knew that she could rewrite the past in order to heal the present, so she gave herself a fantasy. Whatever she wished she had, she pretended at that moment that she had it. Brenda's father had died when she was young, so she missed receiving love from a masculine adult figure. She decided she could imagine herself in her dad's warm, loving arms, just the way she had been when she was little. Miraculously, her attraction for the man she'd gone out with was gone as soon as she tried this imaginative technique the first time.

The exercise Brenda did allowed her to tap into her masculine side. Brenda realized that what she really needed from the man she met was within herself. She also learned that Spirit, or Life, gave her everything she needed when she looked carefully and opened herself to love.

Now Brenda is able to gain the love she needs from the male side of herself and from God by pretending she already has it. She has learned to give love to herself in a healthy, creative way.

And this story has an even happier ending. Now Brenda is attracting men who are emotionally mature and can be stable and steadfast friends. Not only that, she has become a therapist who trains other therapists to do inner-child work with their clients, and she loves her life!

Brenda's story illustrates how the subconscious mind works—in images. Whatever images we create by our very powerful imaginations go directly into our subconscious minds to be created. Therefore, if you think, *I'm not loved*, you lose the ability to perceive the love that surrounds and fills you constantly. If you state "I'm *always* loved," imagine it, and believe it, the love will come from every direction. It will come through a child, a pet, a friend, or the very ethers.

MAKE COMMITMENTS TO YOURSELF

First of all, pat yourself on the back for having a good level of commitment to yourself right now. *You're reading this book*, so you are obviously the kind of person who feels you are worthy of being kind to yourself and waking yourself up to new and wonderful possibilities. Congratulations!

If you have done even one of the exercises in this book for loving yourself, you can give yourself two pats on the back. You're already on your way to more joy and love.

Have you met folks who had trouble making commitments to others?

I was one of those people.

Even though I thought none of the men I met could make commitments, I was actually the one. I know, because nearly all of these noncommittal men got married to the next girlfriend they had!

Now I realize that I didn't even like the word *commitment* back then. It sounded to me like something from a mental hospital.

I noticed some time ago that I was not attracting any committed relationships because I hadn't made any sort of real commitment to *myself.* Boy, oh boy, was this a revelation!

Since then I have made quite a bit of progress, beginning small. I started out with plants. (Don't laugh. Plants aren't easy for me to keep alive.) Taking care of my plants daily made me aware that I needed to take some attention off myself and care for something which would give in return.

I made a commitment to my teddy bears. I told them I would never part with them. Believe it or not, this was a big step for me! I had always given them away and bought new ones whenever I moved to a new city.

Ah, yes, new cities—that brought up a big commitment issue for me. I decided to actually settle down and make a commitment to a city. I liked Portland better than anywhere I'd been, so I decided to live there and settle there.

What about family?

Since I seemed to shy away subconsciously from anyone to whom I would have to make a promise, I decided to get a cat. I promised her that we would always be family. That was a tough one, even though she was so easy to take care of. Actually, I think that she took care of me more than I took care of her.

Friends were another step. I could have really good friends if I could find a way to keep them for life. I met some great friends in Portland. These were friends who were definitely willing to make lifetime commitments to always be friends and always be there for each other in times of need. I felt as though I had a new family—one that I could rely on and one that could rely on me.

Then I finally discovered the man of my dreams. He

was someone I'd known for years as a friend. I hadn't recognized him before as the perfect man for me because I
wasn't ready to accept commitment or give it in return. He
was so fully able to make commitments that he decided to
move to Portland, sight unseen, just because *I* was living
there, and marry me because he knew it was right!

It feels good to have taken all the steps to get here,
now that I look back, even though I know there are always
more to take. I'm committed to myself now, and to doing
what is in my best and healthiest interest, knowing it will
also be best for those around me in many more ways than
I can possibly imagine.

Something You Can Do:

1. Act like a detective. Begin looking for clues as to how
   you can make more of a commitment to yourself.
   Other people give you clues by the way they treat you.
   For example, perhaps someone in your life or work
   lacks the courtesy to let you know that he or she appreciates something nice you did for him or her. Write
   about the situation in your journal in one or two para-
   graphs. Include all of your feelings about it.

2. Choose one key phrase to condense your feelings.
   Write the word or phrase in your journal. If you were
   writing feelings about the example above, they might
   be, "Treated unkindly," or "No appreciation."

3. Now ask yourself a question, related to the phrase you
   just wrote, about how you may treat yourself this

same way. Here are some examples: "How am I un-
kind to *myself*?" or "Do I appreciate *myself* enough?"

4. Find a way to be kinder to or more considerate of
   yourself. You could, for example, buy higher quality
   clothing, which would actually last longer and look
   better. You could eat healthier, better quality food;
   pay greater attention to health care and exercise; or
   simply smile at yourself and be aware that you have
   done a good job, no matter what anyone else says.

❤ ❤ ❤

Everyone in life mirrors how we treat ourselves. So we
can easily see how to love ourselves more by watching
how others treat us. I used to be very hard on myself, so
others were just as hard on me! I even felt criticized when
someone merely tried to make a suggestion.

Here's what I do now: I make it a game. When I'm
really irritated with someone I love or the person who
has just criticized me, I pose these questions: What is life
trying to tell me about myself? Am I being too critical of
myself?

I know that each and every situation is really a gift
from life to teach me how to be happier, whether or not
I choose to see it that way.

LOVE YOURSELF ENOUGH TO SAY "NO" WHEN YOU WANT TO

A young man named George, whom everyone thought of as sweet, kind, and helpful, was on his way to the beach one day to take a restful walk and relax. He was just getting ready to leave the house and thinking how wonderful this day of recuperation would be after all his hard work and study. Just then, a neighbor came over and asked him to help out with an especially tough tree branch he was trying to cut down.

Automatically, George said, "Oh, sure!" It didn't even cross his mind to say, "I'm sorry, but my day is full."

A feeling of disappointment surfaced and was suppressed. He had to cut short his much-needed relaxation time.

George was almost addicted to helping others and found little time for himself. Because he needed love so much, he couldn't possibly turn down an opportunity to prove that he was lovable. Of course, he didn't realize that it was love he was looking for in the praise and thanks he'd get.

After two hours of working on cutting down three tree branches, George felt exhausted and hungry. He no longer had time or energy for the quiet walk on the beach he'd so desperately needed. The next day he came down with a severe cold and was unable to work or go to school. He lost money from not working and had to study extra hours to make up for missed classes. His health became worse.

George learned from that experience to say "No." He learned to love himself enough to take care of himself.

Who else would do it?

No one, he discovered, was more able to know what he needed than he was. If he wasn't strong and healthy, how could he be of service to anyone else when it was truly needed?

The other thing George realized is that both the neighbor and his trees would have been ultimately happier with a professional tree trimmer.

When people feel like saying "No," but say "Yes" anyway, they are doing everyone around them a disservice. I know, because I did it for years and I still have to watch this tendency in myself.

When you decide to work on getting "No" into your vocabulary more often and your family isn't understanding your new tack, try telling them that you're filling your bucket of love so you have more to give them when they really need it.

There are many times I have said "Yes" to a favor, realizing later that I really wanted to say "No." Now when that happens, I give myself permission to call the person back and say: "I have realized that I'm overextending myself and that it's not going to work for me at this time. Is there someone else who might be able to help you out?" Now when someone asks me for a favor, I've also trained myself to say: "I need to think about that. May I get back to you?"

Something You Can Do:

Ask a friend or family member to help you practice this technique:

1. Have the person ask you for a mock favor. For example, your friend says, "Will you drive me to the store?" or "Will you help me wash the car?"

2. Say to the person, "Let me think about it." Or just say, "I'm sorry; I won't be able to do that for you this time." You might also give other suggestions or suggest other people to help, if the asker seems distraught.

3. Continue to practice saying, "Let me think about it," every time someone asks you to do something.

HOW DOES IT HELP OTHERS WHEN YOU TRUTHFULLY ANSWER "NO"?

One day my good friend Jenny called to ask if I would give her a ride to the garage to pick up her newly repaired car. I was facing a book deadline at the time, managing the production of a large seminar, volunteering for Junior Achievement at a local school, working every day, and allowing myself to be generally overextended.

Now, Jenny was one of my best friends, but it seemed she needed more favors than I could possibly give at that time in my life. I'd helped her out the week before, as had her other friends. I just knew it would be unhealthy for me to give more. My health was on the edge, as well.

Since the book deadline was confidential, Jenny didn't even know I was working on it. This made me feel bad about saying "No." It was the first time I'd ever refused to help a friend, and I felt terrible. But I knew it was vital for me to respect my own feelings about the situation.

So I said to her: "Jenny, I'm really sorry, but I'm just not able to do this now. Perhaps something will work out that's just right." She said she didn't know anyone else who could help her that day, and she was very upset with me. She didn't have much money, so she felt helpless and hurt. She didn't call me for nearly a month. I was very upset, because I thought I'd lost her friendship.

Jenny finally called a few weeks after the request to tell me what had happened after I told her I couldn't give her a ride. She was really steamed for a while, but then she realized that I did her an even bigger favor.

She discovered that *she could take care of herself.*

She was so frustrated about always having to feel dependent on others whenever she felt stranded. She came up with a brilliant solution that may seem obvious to you but had never before occurred to her. She decided to call a cab and put the ride on her credit card!

She told me that because of my being able to say "No" when I needed to do so for myself, she was able to say "Yes" to herself and her own independence. Jenny said she found a strength inside herself that she didn't even know she had! If I had relented and said "Yes" when she sounded so helpless, I would have hurt two people, not just one. I would have hurt myself by stretching way too thin, possibly causing worse health, exhaustion, and added stress. And I would have hurt Jenny by not allowing her the freedom she needed to become more creative and independent.

Today Jenny is stronger, freer, braver, and much more independent than she ever could have imagined. She decided to find an apartment of her own, by herself, for the first time in her life. When her son left home, she faced her loneliness with rare grace and courage.

Jenny continues to find ways to strengthen herself physically, emotionally, and spiritually. She also found a new love and moved to a new city where she knew no one but him, taking yet another step for freedom and independence.

Was it all because I said "No"?

Probably not. But I believe this experience made a difference in the way Jenny moved forward in her life. It also made a huge difference in my own life. I discovered the world could still go on if I said "No."

I still struggle with saying "No" to things, because just like everyone else, I want to be loved. If I'm honest with myself, I realize that being loved is the most important thing in the world to me.

But now I realize more than ever that people love me most when I am true to myself. Those seem to be the times I feel God's love most too.

I do the best I can to follow my heart, and I know that if *you* do so too, you'll be a happier person for it. If you can recognize God's love in those moments, you will be filled with more love than you may ever have known.

WHAT ELSE WORKS FOR LEARNING TO GIVE OURSELVES LOVE?

If you have a desire to fill your life with more love, you'll find ways to do this simply by looking for them. Be creative and make up your own Loving Yourself Exercises. Watch your life and your responses to see what new ways you can find to love yourself more.

The greatest thing you can do to give yourself love is to *believe* that you are loved. And you *are*. Give yourself the love you deserve, every day, every moment you can think of love. We are told that God loves us, so why not believe it? Accepting this statement is one way you can move forward.

What helped me most was finding out that we *exist* because God loves us. God's love is an eternal, all-encompassing, unconditional love. If we truly want to experience this love, we need to stop struggling long enough to feel it.

CHAPTER 5

Love Yourself as You Love Your Neighbor

MOST OF US ARE WELL AWARE of the popular phrase from the Bible, "Love your neighbor as yourself." Perhaps the reason there is such a scarcity of love for others in our world these days is this: People do not often love themselves. Love your neighbor as yourself. When people love themselves more, they have more love to give others, even in less-than-friendly circumstances.

HOW CAN YOU LOVE YOURSELF ENOUGH TO TRULY LOVE OTHERS?

When you love others, you're really only loving a reflection of yourself. The more you love the parts of yourself that are crying for attention, the more love you can give those same qualities in others. Also, you'll find that others give you more love and that you'll receive it more easily. How does this work?

When my husband does something that makes me react in anger or hurt feelings, I try to look at what may be causing the reaction within myself and give it love. For example, like most women, I like to know I look pretty when getting dressed up to go out. My husband may or may not comment. I have at least three choices.

First choice: I can assume he doesn't notice how I look and be hurt, meaning I am having negative thoughts about myself by accepting his silence as a negative view of me.

Second choice: I can ask him what he thinks of my outfit. He is always complimentary, though he's a man of few words. He will generally say, "You look nice." From the intonation, inflection, and body language, I can use my imagination to glean further meaning.

Third choice: I can take my attention off myself, knowing I look great, and give *him* a compliment!

ARE WE BEING UNKIND TO OURSELVES?

Often in life we may feel that others mistreat us by being unfair, rude, critical, and so on. By paying attention to our emotional and mental reactions to these situations, we can become more and more cognizant of our own unfair, rude, and critical thoughts toward ourselves.

I've had experiences of giving love to myself and a friend or mate in times when emotions surfaced. I found that the love came back to me and changed me. Often the other person changed too, but sometimes it was necessary to let go of the relationship anyway. Once I learned everything I could from it, I woke up to my true potential.

One such situation occurred with an acquaintance I had long ago. A woman we will call "Wanda" got very angry at me whenever I voiced my own feelings about what I needed, if it conflicted with *her* plans. Knowing that her anger was likely a reflection of something within me, some part of me which needed attention, I looked inside and tried to see what it was. It seemed as though she was very reactive. I could see myself getting fearful when she reacted in anger. The little girl inside me was remembering the beatings my older brother and sister used to get when my grandfather got very angry.

The solution was to give that frightened little girl inside me some love and attention. Also, if I could give my friend that same love, knowing she was simply acting out a part of my life, perhaps it would help. I worked on this theory for a few weeks. What happened was surprising to me. Wanda actually became angrier! One day when I responded with genuine concern to her request for a loan and said, "Let me think about it," she reacted angrily and hung up the phone!

Wanda did not call back for a long time. We finally saw each other and talked it out, but she still could not seem to let go of the anger. I decided simply to stop pursuing the friendship in any active way. I stopped calling her or inviting her to do things with me, although I was very pleasant and friendly if I happened to see her somewhere.

The friendship eventually dissipated on its own, because I resolved the fear in me and she was not able to do the same with her anger. A good rule of thumb is that if you change your own attitudes, the other person changes or disappears. In this case, Wanda could not change to match my change, so she had to move out of my circle of activity and friendship.

Something You Can Do NOW:

1. Write in your journal all of the mean, cruel words you say to yourself on a regular basis. An example: "I'm so stupid!"

2. Look at the list as if your best friend or neighbor had written it to you.

3. Cross out the words you would never tolerate from others. I hope they are all crossed out when you have finished!

4. Make a vow right now to notice when you say these words to yourself mentally. You know the power of affirmation. You do not want these limiting affirmations. Each time you catch them, replace them with positive, opposite affirmations such as this: *I'm a vehicle for God in my life. Everything I do has a divine purpose that will unfold in time.*

HOW CAN WE BE GOOD TO OURSELVES WHEN OTHERS MISTREAT US?

A young man met a famous author and fell in love with her. They lived together for eighteen years, during which time he realized that she verbally abused him fairly regularly. It was so subtle that it undermined his self-esteem slowly, like water wearing on a stone. He didn't realize this until many years into the relationship.

He finally decided to walk away. That was the very best thing he could do for his self-esteem. After years of research and writing, he is now well respected as *the* expert on self-esteem. His name is Nathaniel Branden, and you may want to take a look at some of his books on self-esteem if you feel you need to strengthen yours.

Reading Mr. Branden's story made me realize that one very important thing I could do to improve my self-esteem was to walk away from situations which were destroying what little self-worth I did feel. I'm so grateful now, as I look back, that I was able to walk away from relationships which subtly wore away at my confidence.

I know that most difficult relationships don't dissolve easily. However, I have found that if we can somehow change ourselves or how we *think* about ourselves, the other person will often move right along with us or go his or her own way, as Wanda did. If it is too difficult to move out of a bad situation on your own, get help.

Help is out there for any of us who is willing to spend the money. Yes, I said "spend the money"! How much do you spend on car payments, car insurance, and car repairs every month so that your vehicle will get you where you need and want to go in life?

Are *you* worth that much?

Of course you are, and much, much more! If your car is carrying around an unhappy person, it's not going to help to put more money into your car. The same goes for your house, clothes, vacations, or sports equipment. And if you think that new cars, clothes, face-lifts, muscles, or any other physical things will make you more lovable, don't waste your money. Get counseling from a professional highly recommended by someone you trust.

If you truly cannot afford therapy and you know you need it, find a service organization or university that can help you for free or very little money.

If you've done all the talk therapy and found it to be a dead end for you, you may find that a kind of therapy which works on a deep, subconscious level can be effective. This can be especially true if you are, like me, good at fooling therapists into thinking that you are perfectly happy with yourself and that you don't *really* have any deep-seated issues. Also, check into "Solution-Oriented Therapy," which is the theme of the book *Fire Your Shrink!* by Michele Weiner-Davis.

Pray, contemplate, or meditate about it and ask God for help, in whatever way you pray to God, and you *will* know what to do. Trust yourself to listen to the highest within you, and know that you are a child of God, loved by God always, for you are a sparkling, bright, and loving soul!

Seeing the Good in Yourself Helps You Love Others Even More

It used to be difficult for me to see the good in myself as others saw it. I was always so surprised when someone complimented me. I still feel a little funny, but I do my best to accept the compliments gracefully and to look at myself from the complimenter's viewpoint. I am not encouraging narcissism, but I do feel it's important to understand that even though we're not better than others, we *are* just as good!

If you're having difficulty seeing the good in yourself, try this next journaling technique.

Something You Can Do NOW:

1. Get out your journal and write at the top of a page, "What do I feel good about in myself?" Then write whatever you can think of. Write the things that make you feel good when you do them, whether it is helping others, doing volunteer work, or opening doors for others.

2. Leave some room on that page to add to it later, as you think of things, and on the next page write at the top, "What do other people like about me?" Now write all the compliments you can remember on this one page, and keep going if you need to use more pages!

3. Whenever you need a boost, read the above pages or post them somewhere private.

LOVE YOURSELF BY *EXPECTING* LOVE IN YOUR LIFE

Little "Rebecca" knew that every single person, place, animal, and plant in her life was put there by God and was giving her love all the time. She knew, because her guardian angel said so. People would laugh at her for smiling all the time. Her mother wondered what she was up to! Rebecca was such a trusting soul that her brother used to tell her she was just too gullible. He pulled pranks on her all the time. Funny thing was, she didn't mind when people laughed at her. They seemed to laugh the most when Rebecca was trying to be serious and philosophical. That was okay, she figured, since people were happy when they laughed. Why shouldn't they enjoy themselves? She knew they loved her anyway, silly as she seemed to them.

When Rebecca grew up, she traveled around the country and learned about the many different cultures within her own land. Somehow she was always able to pay the rent and to have lots of good food and wonderful friends. She didn't have a lot, but she always had enough. She believed in serving life and all who came into her life. Life gave her back so much. The only thing missing was a mate. Rebecca became so lonely that she eventually forgot how to love life and let life love her. One day she realized that she was no longer the openhearted, happy child she had been. She decided to watch children.

How did they get through the day?

They let hurtful things go quickly, forgave quickly, and had fun! They sat down if they were tired and said "I'm hungry!" if they needed to eat. They hugged without hesitation. They smiled and laughed for no reason at all, it seemed.

Rebecca decided it was time to learn how to be a child again, with the wisdom gleaned from being an adult to keep her in balance. Life was good again, and all the trees, flowers, animals, and friends loved her again.

Rebecca, like all of us, had a loving, grateful nature and she knew that life was essentially good. She knew that love is the essence of life, if she would just look deeply for it, expecting to find it everywhere she went.

I can relate closely to Rebecca's story, because it reminds me so much of my own. It's easy to forget that love is everywhere, no matter where we are or who is there with us. It is within even when we are alone and feel no love exists at all. All we need to do is recognize its existence and acknowledge its presence.

One thing that helps me tremendously, which I encourage you to try as well, is to *expect* love in your life, as a small child might do with open innocence. Expect it at every turn. Love may come in the most disarming, unexpected, surprising, and subtle ways. A child may smile at you—and that is truly a gift from God. An angel may touch your heart as you feel surrounded by a warm blanket of love. A puppy may stop to tell you with its tongue that you are the most important person in the whole world right now.

Something You Can Do NOW:

1. Experiment by imagining that tomorrow your day will be completely filled with love. Be a child again and look at the world with a new sense of discovery and wonder.

2. Let the love come to you in whatever way it will, keeping your options wide open, from animals, children, friends, or plants. You may even find yourself in tears

watching a television commercial (don't laugh—I have!). Everywhere you go and everyone you see will glow with that love.

3. Pretend you are in an animated movie such as *Fantasia* and your life is magic. Tomorrow will be an extremely special day. When you see what power you have to change your world just by changing your view of it, you'll want to try this more often. There's no limit on love. You can have as much as you can imagine and receive. Try it and see!

BE KIND TO YOURSELF

A very nice man died and went to heaven. At the pearly gates, St. Peter brought him in to see God. The man asked, "Am I in heaven?" God said: "Yes, you were so nice to everyone in your life on earth. There was just one person I was really concerned about. You did not treat him as kindly as the others and even neglected him quite a bit. You did not give him as much understanding, compassion, or love. This one person did not receive much of the patience you were so generous in giving to others in your life."

Completely bewildered, the gentleman racked his brain to think of who that could possibly be! He had been so careful to be kind and good to everyone in his life. Who had he neglected so? God knew what he was thinking, of course, and said, "It was yourself, dear one; it was yourself."

How many times have you been patient and kind to others, not pushing or hurrying them, being understanding and sympathetic with a good friend, generous and loving with your family? How many times have you been so kind and patient with yourself?

Something You Can Do NOW:

1. Write down any area(s) in your life you feel stressed about. It could be health, unhappiness with a job, a relationship, or something else.

2. If *you* were your *best friend* who loved you dearly, what advice would you give yourself? Write it down right now. You may find that as your best friend you would hear yourself saying to see a doctor, find a new job, get out of that abusive relationship, or get professional help.

3. Now make a commitment to yourself to do what your best friend has just advised you to do. You'll never find a friend who is willing to interfere in your life enough to pick you up bodily and take you to seek health care or counseling without your consent. You must depend on yourself to be your *own* best friend. Write a note to yourself right now on your calendar or in your appointment book to do that very thing.

4. If you did not do #3 because you are concerned about the cost, figure out how much you spend on clothes, automobiles, travel, and entertainment, or items to please others. Isn't your core happiness just as important? Doesn't it make sense to take care of your health and well-being first, so you have more joy to give?

❤ ❤ ❤

A woman we'll call "Sarah" had for years been taking care of others in whatever way she could. She loved to cook, so she created wonderful gourmet meals for her friends. She could never seem to find enough money to buy herself badly needed new clothes or shoes, but if a friend was having a birthday, she was sure to find the money to buy a special, costly gift. She'd buy a lovely teddy bear to brighten a sad friend. Price was no object when it came to anyone but herself. If *she* needed health care, she went to the community clinic, where she could pay little. She knew she needed counseling, but could never seem to justify the expense. The extra money just wasn't there when it was needed for herself, or so it seemed.

As Sarah approached middle age, she found it difficult to understand why she had so little. After all, hadn't she given plenty to others? What goes around comes around, doesn't it? "That is true indeed," a little voice inside herself told her, "but you must find more love in your heart for *yourself* if you want to give the most important gift of all to those you love."

"What gift is that?" she wondered. "The gift of divine love," came the answer. "Divine love is the most pure, unconditional love you can offer, but you can only offer it when you need nothing in return. That will happen only when you have filled your own needs first. Then all you have given will come back to you unhindered."

Sarah decided to try giving love to herself and found

it more satisfying than any other gift she could think of. This was a gift that was there whenever she had need or want of it. It could not be used up, and in fact the more she used it, the more she got of it! This could not be said of jewels, fine clothes, or chocolates! Once Sarah was filled to the brim with this divine, unconditional love, she found that she could give many gifts to others without feeling the need to have the favor returned. After all, didn't she already have the greatest gift of all and one that cannot be bought?

Something You Can Do NOW:

1. List what you do readily for others.

2. Ask yourself how many items on the list of what you do for others you would have liked others to do for you in return. Write what they are.

3. Choose one of those things to do for yourself. Put it on your calendar, and make a date with yourself to do that very thing. Sign it and commit to it, as if you were making an appointment with your best friend (you are!).

Try to have as much love and compassion for yourself as you do for your loved ones. Try to *be* one of your loved ones. Try to *love yourself as you love your neighbor*. Then you will be able to "love your neighbor as yourself."

CHAPTER 6

Conquering Blocks to Loving Yourself

NOW THAT YOU HAVE BEGUN to experiment with some new ways to love yourself, you may have noticed some old emotions surfacing. They may be calling to you to go back to the way things were, to a comfort zone where they were unthreatened. Filling yourself with more love could move them to the surface and right out on their keisters!

Hang in there and face those old, no-longer-necessary acquaintances. Fight them with the most powerful thing you've got—love.

WHAT ARE THE DRAGONS THAT BLOCK THE GATEWAY TO LOVE?

There are so many different blocks to loving ourselves that I may not think of the ones you've experienced. Because each of us is such a unique combination of personality, experience, and individual soul, each of our dragons is going to look different from anyone else's. And of course, we have more than one. I think that when I began this process I had about twelve! Here's a sampling of some that different people may have:

FEARS:

- Fear of rejection
- Fear of not being loved
- Fear of losing personal identity
- Fear of being hurt again

FEELINGS OF UNWORTHINESS:

- Feeling unworthy of love
- Feeling guilty about being too happy, feeling too much love
- Feeling low self-esteem

OLD BELIEFS:

- Old ideas about self-denial, work ethics, and so on
- Old parental "tapes" in your head

This list could go on, but the easiest way to look for the blocks is to look for the fear and other related emotions. Be aware of what you are feeling in various uncomfortable situations. Act as if you were an observer, or witness. Watch yourself breathe (or *not* breathe!). See if your throat tightens or your solar plexus (belly) gets tight and anxious. Does your heart pound? Do you feel afraid, angry, resentful, guilty?

Whatever emotion you feel, fear is the root emotion

that underlies almost every emotional block to loving ourselves or accepting love from others, even from God. Are
you ready to start knocking out some of those old fears?
If so, keep reading and try some of the exercises that relate to fears and other blocks which you recognize as
being your dragons. Just being aware of the blocks that
you have will help resolve them.

BLOCK #1—FEARS

We humans have a strong tendency toward the emotion of fear. Why? Fear is our protection. It keeps us alive
when we are threatened by the unknown. If we've been
hurt, physically or verbally abused, threatened, rejected,
or abandoned, we have likely built a wall of protection to
keep out the threat of further pain, as a natural instinct for
emotional survival. The downside is that this fear may
also keep us from experiencing greater love.

Replace Fear with Love

How can we get rid of the fear that keeps us from experiencing love? We can replace it with love. It has been
said in many spiritual texts that where there is fear, there
can be no love, and where there is love, there can be no
fear.

One type of fear that keeps us from feeling more love
is the fear of not being loved. Though I was not aware of
it most of my life, this was my greatest fear.

Almost all of my life I believed my mother did not love
me or trust me. I felt resentful that she could not accept

me or my lifestyle, my choice of religion, boyfriend, car, or even hairstyle! I was not what she hoped I would be. That hurt, so of course, I shut her out.

At some point, as I was learning to love myself more, I realized suddenly that I couldn't accept *her* for who *she* was or accept *her* lifestyle either! I thought this would be a good place to start, so I began to accept her more. Miraculously, I could feel that it freed *me* as well.

I came to the conclusion that no one had ever shown *her* how to express love or trust. Her parents had died when she was two years old. Raised by hard-working grandparents and a stern maiden aunt, my adoptive mother was an emotional orphan herself. She simply didn't have the tools, the experience, or the means to find the love to pass along to me. She loved me, but she could not seem to express that love in words or actions.

Once I began to work on loving myself more, I had more to give. I was filled with more love, so I could give some to her, even though she was still unable to express it much with me. Over the years I kept giving to myself and to her as well. There was plenty to go around, once I found a way to "tap the source."

After a few years, my mother began to tell me that she loved me too and that she was proud of me. She lent a sympathetic ear when my heart got broken or things didn't work out well. She was never effusive, but I began to look for love in the little things, and I knew, finally, that she really *did* love me.

I had to overcome my own fears by filling myself with love, then I could see clearly the love that had always been there for me. Is this something you would like to experience too?

Something You Can Do NOW:

When feeling fear of rejection, being alone, or not being loved, you can imagine your way out! There is no need to continue to feel like a victim. Get out your journal and begin to write:

1. Choose a situation in which you often find yourself feeling rejected, lonely, criticized, unloved, or challenged in some similar way. Write the story with all the feeling you can muster. Really dramatize it.

   Some of those feelings come from a very deep place and are perfectly valid. (If it feels as if your emotions are getting out of hand and affecting your life negatively, definitely see a professional counselor or therapist.)

2. Read over your story as if it were someone else's and you were looking for clues, like a good investigator. Look for any emotion that might be lurking underneath the fear. It could be anger, sadness, grief, or something else. Also, look at what specific fear it may be, such as abandonment, abuse, or rejection.

3. Acknowledge that you feel this way when you are challenged by this particular situation.

   Assume that by your awareness it no longer has the power over you it had before. You're the one in control. You have faced the dragon and moved toward it.

4. Continue taking control of the situation by imagining yourself feeling more comfortable in the situation the next time you're in it. (To stay balanced in life, do *not* try to change the other people who may be involved, only how *you* might feel or behave.)

Imagine you are completely comfortable and happy as you see, hear, or feel yourself back there again. Ask for love and guidance from your higher Self or God. Know that you are choosing to "change the channel" on this program, and do it!

Here's how this exercise worked for a woman I will call "Cindy." Often feeling very lonely and fearing rejection, Cindy decided one evening to make a dramatic change. As she sat on her couch alone, crying and surrounded by cookies and chips, Cindy realized that she could change her viewpoint and thus change her experience. She knew a lot of people, and she liked them. She wondered what it would be like if they were all at her house right then, having a party. That would feel so good!

She then closed her eyes and imagined herself in the midst of all this love and joy, surrounded by good friends who were hugging her. Cindy told me that she also remembered to feel grateful for their love. Gratitude is a quality of life that makes magic happen.

Suddenly Cindy's phone started ringing off the hook! People she hadn't heard from in years began to call. Cindy was elated.

All Cindy had done was change her attitude from one of feeling sorry for herself to one of having all the love she wanted—and miracle of miracles, she actually then had it! Cindy has not allowed herself the luxury of feeling sorry for herself since; she knows it's really not a luxury at all, but a very detrimental attitude.

I can relate to Cindy's story, because I felt lonely for most of my life. I would ask myself and God what I was doing wrong. One day I faced my fear of loneliness and said to it, "Okay, fear, just *be* there. I'm going to go on with my life and enjoy it the best way I can, looking for love wherever I can find it." I looked for love in fragrant flowers, the evening chorus of songbirds, the smile of thanks I received from opening doors for "golden age" ladies, my sweet kitties, and even some favorite television shows. It worked! The biggest part of the loneliness went away, and I was happy being alone most of the time and feeling more and more love each day.

When we look for love, it's truly there. Though I was still alone for many years, I found the experience to be a wonderful lesson in finding love in the most subtle of circumstances. Necessity *does* make one very creative!

Would you like to take the plunge and get to the bottom of your fear? Bring it to the surface and let it float away with the exercise below.

One More Thing You Can Do:

1. Write down the fear or block that you think may be getting in the way of your experiencing more love.

2. Ask God or your guardian angel for a dream that will help you better understand how to get through this block.

3. When you wake up, write down everything you can remember, even if it's just one word. *You* will know what it means. Trust that you will get the answer you need.

4. Repeat this dream exercise every night until you remember something. Always pick up a pen and paper in the morning, even if you remember nothing. Give this thirty days if necessary. It can take awhile or require several dreams, if you are not yet ready for the answer.

BLOCK #2—FEELINGS OF UNWORTHINESS

How is feeling unworthy a block to love? Feeling unworthy of love blocks love because it makes us sabotage ourselves. We won't attract true, committed love if we feel too much guilt or low self-esteem. These feelings often stem from negative parental comments, negative childhood experiences, put-downs, and various other experiences that create low self-esteem.

Up until very recently, I still had a difficult time thinking *I am worthy of love.* However, I truly believe all of God's creatures are worthy of love. Am I not one of them? On rare occasions, still, there are times I exclude myself from that universal group, because I do have occasional doubts about being worthy of love. All we can do when that happens is continue to focus on who we really are inside and know that, as the Self, we are here because we came from love and because every single one of us is part of that love right now.

What makes people feel worthy of love?

Would You Be More Worthy of Love if
YOU WERE RICH AND FAMOUS?

I doubt that being rich or famous automatically makes people feel more worthy of love. In fact, I *know* it doesn't. There have been many unhappy people among history's most famous.

I doubt that Marilyn Monroe killed herself because she was happy or because she felt loved. Nor did others in her shoes. There is a lot of loneliness that comes with being "at the top," because people still have to face themselves wherever they are! Fame and riches do not bring more love and never will.

When I had the most money in my life, I was the loneliest. Learning to find my self-worth as a spiritual being was what finally made me feel worthy of love.

Would You Be Worthy of More Love if
YOUR PARENTS FINALLY VALIDATED YOU?

"Louise" found out she had to discover her own value once she realized her parents could never give it to her. She was the oldest of nine children and was often given the parenting role, whether she wanted it or not. When she tried to excel in some way, her parents resented it, feeling she was breaking away from the family and her responsibilities.

When Louise came home from school with a glowing

report card, her parents made comments like, "Well, if they knew you as we know you, they would never have given you these good grades." Louise's parents had found a way to put her down again, keeping her just where they wanted her. This convinced Louise that she should never let her light shine and that she really wasn't worthy of anything greater.

Louise grew up believing that if anyone ever found out who she really was, they would know she was not worthy. She finally found ways—through therapy, spiritual exercises, and her religion—to overcome these feelings of unworthiness. Louise knows now that she *is* the light which shines forth from her and that she can validate herself without the approval of her parents or anyone else.

Would You Be Worthy Of More Love if YOU WORKED HARDER AND LONGER?

I used to fall into this trap. I subconsciously thought that if I worked hard, I then deserved to play. Otherwise, I felt guilty. I felt more worthwhile when I was productive rather than just "there," without getting anything done. Then I learned that overworking was symptomatic of feelings of unworthiness. I realized I needed to love myself enough to moderate the workload.

Now when I relax and decide I will get everything done in just a few hours, I do! I also make more money when I do this.

Whatever you subconsciously agree to, others around you will agree to as well, subconsciously. If you agree to overwork, they will gladly agree that you must overwork by giving you more work, not less.

Some people overwork because they are lonely and simply want to fill the time or avoid feeling their pain. However, the work takes over and such people become unbalanced in "all work and no play." They then have no time to take care of or love themselves, and therefore no one else (who is healthy and functional) will love or take care of them either—an endless cycle.

If you find yourself in this predicament, take time to meet others through classes, clubs, associations, organizations, and volunteer activities. It may sound like work to you if you are already overworked, but it will actually help you balance your time between work and play a little better. Volunteer work is relaxing for most people, according to some experts.

Also, spending more time with yourself to process old emotions, become aware of and release old fears and beliefs, and daydream about your new goals is vital to moving forward. Give yourself a minivacation (a day at the beach or in the mountains) away from everyone and everything and see how light you feel afterward!

Remember the magic of your divine gift, imagination. We have free will to imagine anything we want, and Holy Spirit fills these images with life. So imagine you have time for yourself and your loved ones. Imagine relaxing and enjoying your life more, and you will find ways and means coming to you on silent cat's paws or blaring bugles. It doesn't matter, as long as it happens.

When you decide to take better care of yourself, so will

others. It's magical! Self-respect gains others' respect. It seems impossible, but it makes total sense. Never underestimate the power of your attitude about yourself to influence others.

Expect to Be Treated With Respect and Settle for Nothing Less

A lack of self-esteem caused me to settle for less than what was available to me in all aspects of my life. Once I discovered I could have more love in my life, I asked God to help me find the highest and the best in every department of my life, from career to relationships. I wanted to be treated with respect and kindness. The spiritual being you are deserves the very best too. Here's an example of someone else who thought so, once he saw the light.

"William" continued to spend money on "Sharon," which he did gladly, even though she remained uncommitted to even a close friendship. Not calling when she said she would and canceling dates at the last minute was a continual habit for her. This reminded William of his mother, who he felt had neglected him as a child.

After a year of this kind of treatment from Sharon, William decided to break the pattern. Since he couldn't seem to reach her in person and she was not returning his calls, William left Sharon a message saying he would no longer tolerate this inconsiderate behavior. He said that if she wanted his friendship, she would have to respect it.

William did not hear from Sharon for nearly two months, in which time he wondered if he had been a bit too harsh. Still, he felt better about himself than he had in many months. Finally, Sharon called him and told him she would be more respectful of him and their friendship, which she missed. She explained that she knew this behavior of not being committed was a pattern for her and said that she wanted to be more considerate of her friends now.

Sharon has been true to her word, and she and William have remained good friends.

William has grown up emotionally and realizes that Sharon is not the mate for him, but is a valuable friend, even as he dates other women. He has let go of his attachment to Sharon, because he realized that, on a subconscious level it reminded him of his relationship with his mother. William realized that Sharon was there to teach him a lesson: the lesson that his friendship is just as valuable as anyone's and that he deserves to be treated kindly and with consideration.

William also learned from this experience that he deserves to receive as well as to give and that when he gives in personal relationships, it must be balanced by the other person's giving too. Now William is attracting women who return his attention and interest because he has more self-esteem and self-respect and a much better self-image.

Can you relate to that story? *I* certainly can. I've seen big changes in my relationships since I have learned to let go of friendships that are one-sided and of people who disrespect the commitments they have made. I slowly improved by recognizing sooner and sooner the lack of commitment or respect in relationships, and as soon as I did realize it, I let go and moved on. I also decided not to settle for anything less than what I knew I wanted. You can too!

Something You Can Do:

1. Take a look at your friendships and relationships of various kinds. Jot down a few notes in your journal about some of these relationships. What qualities did they have that you liked? Didn't like?

   Ask yourself if you would treat a person the way you have been treated by your friends, family, and associates. If the answer is "Yes, I have been treated kindly," then skip the rest of this exercise. If the answer is "No, I have not been treated kindly," then proceed.

2. Do you treat others kindly? Then you deserve to be treated well in return. Take a moment to think of how you might move toward other friendships and let go of the ones that don't serve you as well as you serve them. This doesn't have to happen abruptly. Simply taking your attention off these people and placing it on people who return your affections kindly will open the doors to new friendships. The old ones that you'd rather not keep will often fall away naturally.

3. Know that you will instantly improve your self-esteem by doing so. Sometimes it's the only way. For more on this, see *The Six Pillars of Self-Esteem* by Nathaniel Branden.

❤ ❤ ❤

Another true story is about a man who waited years for a woman who was alternately hot and cold. One minute she was his friend, the next minute she was his lover, then back to being his friend again. He never wavered in his friendship for her, yet his heart broke as he watched her date other men, because he felt he was truly the one for her. Finally, he tried the exercise of filling the pain with blue light and singing HU, the love song to God.

Over the next two weeks, he began to get his self-esteem back. He saw clearly that he had to move on with his own life. The pain subsided and he was happy again. Then a miracle occurred. She came back to him and was ready to make a commitment. Now he was a full and healthy man, and she knew it.

People can sense when we are empty inside—needy and desperate for love. I know this from personal experience. I was all of those things most of my life. It took me years, but I healed the pain through spending a lot of time with myself and with others who could help me.

I also used the spiritual exercise with blue light and HU. It worked! I feel "in love" most of the time, just being human and being willing to receive the love that's there for us all. Now, when my husband is out of town or having his "cave time," I no longer feel abandoned. I feel good about myself and my life, and I feel loved.

BLOCK #3—OLD BELIEFS

We all have beliefs about love that are good. We also have beliefs that may limit us. These beliefs may come from our peers, parents, media, or some authority figure. They can affect us very deeply. They're buried in our subconscious minds, directing what we expect from life and therefore receive.

Some of these beliefs have to do with God's love; some have to do with *human* love. I know I have had untrue beliefs about both.

For a few years (well, okay, for *all* of my life up to very recently) I believed that I was unlovable. This was probably caused by having felt abandoned and rejected in my early childhood, as I have explained. Quite unconsciously, I felt unworthy and unloved. I wondered if my friends really wanted to spend much time with me! I had no idea that I felt or believed these things. I just kept doing such an inappropriate number of nice things for people I cared about that I scared people away. Either they couldn't keep up with me, or it made them feel uncomfortable. I was doing those things to earn their love, which I already had and didn't even know it.

Subconsciously, I must have believed I was somehow not good enough all by myself. I had to come bearing gifts to be worthy of their affection and attention. I had to do great and wonderful favors, be smart and successful, drive a nice car, and make sure I wasn't in the way! I had to act in a manner that my loved ones wanted me to act. That was my unconscious belief.

Of course, how my dear ones wanted me to act was probably just to be myself. I, however, assumed that "just being myself" could never be good enough. I had to please everyone but myself in order to win the prize that seemed so far out of reach to me—love. Remember that this was all going on subconsciously. I had no idea I didn't believe I was loved until I took a good look at my behavior. I didn't trust my friends to simply love me for myself. I was actually being given the love I so desperately needed, but I was too busy *giving* desperately to be able to receive it!

All of this was going on even after I had begun the process of learning to love myself and learning to accept a small part of God's love for me. At least I'd been able to pry open a small crack in my heart to let in some badly needed sunshine. I had to concentrate on it, though. It still felt like a struggle to me, after all this time and work!

Then one day I had an idea. Why not try an exercise to feel *worthy* of love, to *believe* I was loved? I began to practice viewing myself more as a spiritual being, and just as good as anyone else. Not better, not worse, but just as good and just as worthy of love. If God loves everyone, then I am included in that too, and so are you!

You are a spiritual being. However you view that, you're a special someone wearing a physical body like an overcoat. When you can see your true, loving Self, then you will see your true beauty. Then you will recognize that you are constantly receiving God's love. Unsteady belief will have long gone and been replaced with a deep, satisfying sense of knowing.

Like others, I'm very hard on myself when I forget who I am and why I'm here. I'm here to grow and unfold my higher Self. I believe that earth is like a school in which we're constantly learning how to be more loving beings. If you wish to know more about who you are as divine, read

Linda C. Anderson's book *35 Golden Keys to Who You Are & Why You're Here*. Reading this book gave me an even fuller perspective on how truly special each of us is.

Do You Believe What You Want Does Exist?

"Grace" also had an old belief about not being able to have what she wanted. Grace wanted to get married. Being a spiritually directed person, she deeply desired a spiritually directed marriage. For her this meant a relationship in which she and her husband had a sense of equality and responsibility toward each other, and a desire to use the marriage as a path within itself, a way of achieving their spiritual goals. If she could just find someone who was mutually committed to spiritual growth in marriage and committed to himself, as she was to herself spiritually, then she would be in heaven!

There was only one challenge, but it was a big one— Grace had never seen or heard of such a relationship. She had no role model for such a relationship. Since she had never seen such a marriage, she feared it didn't exist.

Grace decided, over time and with some astute observation, that there was no one else around who wanted what she wanted. However, she still wanted to get married. Would she have to give up what she desired most to be married? She began to believe she would. She believed she was alone in her quest for a spiritually imbued marriage.

One day Grace woke up to the idea that she didn't have to settle for the lower drawer. She became very sure of what she wanted. She could hold out for the one person who met her expectations. She could believe, after all, that he *did* exist and that she *would* either meet him, or spend her life on her own spiritual quest.

When Grace did this, magic happened. Of course, it took time for it all to come about, but by changing her belief, Grace changed her life and is now married to a wonderful, gentle, and considerate man who shares her spiritual goals and dreams. He works right along with her on their marriage and their spiritual growth.

LOVING YOURSELF HEALS ALL BLOCKS

As I said at the beginning of this chapter, I won't recognize all the blocks to love there may be. I certainly won't know how it feels for you or how you experience or express your blocks. I do know that loving yourself can dissolve them all. Daily practice of any Loving Yourself Exercise will wear away the walls over time.

Here are two exercises to help you recognize and move through any blocks you may have to love, no matter what they are.

Something You Can Do NOW:

Exercise for discovering blocks to experiencing more love and dissolving them:

1. Breathe in deeply, filling your body with a warm, gentle feeling of peace and contentment in this moment. Breathe in and out a few times, imagining a warm, glowing light filling your body from head to toe. When that is done, imagine you are listening to some relaxing music you love. Hear its gentle melody.

2. After you read the next two parts of this exercise, close your eyes and do them. Think of a wonderful country scene—a relaxing pastoral setting where you are walking toward an old stone wall. Imagine the stone wall has a description of your "block to love" written on it. It may be a feeling rather than actual words, but the words will form themselves as you stand in front of the wall. Ask your higher Self, guardian angel, or God for guidance. It may come later or in a dream.

3. Imagine yourself taking down the wall, stone by stone, until it's easy for you to step over it and move on or until it is completely gone, or use your imagination to eliminate or go around your block.

4. What did you see? If nothing, try again later. Now you can begin to resolve these old limits to your happiness in life. Whether you require therapy or not is up to you. If your therapist recommended this book, you may want to tell your therapist what you experienced in this exercise or others.

You will know, if you pray, meditate, or contemplate about it. Otherwise, try this next exercise to see if you can begin to release the old fear or pain. Your imagination can do wonders!

Something More You Can Do:

1. Imagine that each dragon you are being bothered by has a nameplate around its neck.

2. No matter how ferocious this dragon may seem, try to realize that the power of love is much greater and that you can turn this dragon into a kitten with the simplicity of love. Begin to think of this dragon as a part of you that may be hurting, angry, or scared, like a child who has lost its way and is frightened. Imagine sending out waves of love to your dragon, the kind of love you would give your own child if she/he was lost or hurting. As you do this, you will see a change take place.

3. Watch what happens over time as you do this exercise when you feel lost, angry, or afraid. Write what you notice in your journal. Perhaps the dragon will turn into a smaller, more manageable pet or disappear altogether. Maybe you will be able to face these emotions and even let go of them completely in these situations.

4. Commend yourself for your work and your progress, even if they take awhile—mine sure did!

WHAT HAPPENS NOW?

As you do the exercises in this chapter and in the days or weeks following them, you may feel various emotions surfacing. See if you can feel where these emotions reside in your body. If you could name the place you feel your pain, fear, anger, anxiety, sadness, or other emotion, where would it be located? If could be near your heart, stomach, throat, head, or somewhere else in your body.

Once you know where it is, you can breathe into it with loving light and sound, allowing it to surface and release.

How does this work?

Imagine a pot boiling on the stove. It's hot, so you can't touch it, but it has a lid on it. Soon the pot will boil over. If you take the lid off, the steam can escape and everything stays clean. Emotions work like the liquid in the pot: they are either released, or they boil over!

Any good therapist will tell you this about emotions: Emotions are either experienced and passed off, *or* they are suppressed.

Guess what happens when they are suppressed? They boil over!

So who has suppressed emotions? Almost everyone.

During trauma, our bodies often protect our emotions as well, such as when a car-accident victim goes into shock to numb the pain. The physical pain is usually felt later, if the patient is not sedated. The emotional pain often remains buried until we are ready to feel it. But who wants to feel pain if we don't have to?

The good news is that when you are ready to release emotions, they will come out in some way. The best news is that if you use the above exercises and get professional help for the really powerful emotions, you can lead a much more peaceful, stable, and balanced life.

The only thing I can do is just keep breathing and giving myself and these old fears a lot of love. That works to help me get through the fears quickly and to help them release. The fear of feeling them is what has kept them there this long. Now I try to realize that they are simply emotions—nothing more, nothing less—and that they have absolutely no power over me except what I give them.

Remember how many times you might have suppressed emotions or ignored them; it may take awhile to explore what's inside you. Give yourself time and patience. Take time every day for this if you need to. I certainly did for a whole year! I gave myself all the love I could while going through this process. The exercise of imagining light and sound and love in the painful area of my heart healed the pain, and I've not had it since.

Healing my heart made a huge difference in my relationships. Before that I had such a great need for someone else's love, because it was the only time I didn't feel pain in my heart. I know now that each new beau, at that time in my life, could feel this need oozing out of every pore in my body. I was so sure that I was giving him all the freedom in the world, but he could still feel this incredible ache inside me, I am sure.

When I think about how *I* would react if anyone had felt that needy to me, I'm sure I would have gone running in the other direction very quickly. As it was, whoever I was seeing at the time would intuitively feel my unconscious desperation and find some reason to stay away.

I have learned since then how to give myself that love, and it's so freeing! Also, all of my friendships have improved, and I was able to attract a mate who is balanced, communicative, sensitive, kind, and considerate. It truly is a miracle, and one that *you* can have too.

When you are determined to take the time to make

the relationship with *yourself* better, all the relationships in your life will be better. Also, pat yourself on the back for making enough of a commitment to yourself to even pick up a book like this. If you are seriously looking at yourself and your life as you read this and are doing some of the exercises too, then give yourself a big hug. Congratulations! You are committed to yourself and your future in a way most people don't even think about.

If you feel, as I did in the past, that the feeling of being loved is just too difficult and that you simply cannot reach out for love from anyone, try this next exercise.

Something You Can Do NOW:

1. Begin to imagine there is love all around you and within you. You may want to close your eyes and envision a warm, rosy glow of light, invisible to everyone, but present just the same. This is God's love for you.

2. Feel yourself relaxing into this light, as if it had substance to hold you, just as a mother would lovingly hold her baby. Imagine the warmth of this precious love filling your whole being.

❤ ❤ ❤

Sometimes it takes discipline, strange as that may sound, to be able to receive love. It also takes imagination. Can you imagine that God loves *you* as much as God loves anyone else? Can you imagine that this love surrounds you always?

Set aside a special time of day—even as little as one to five minutes will do.

Use the time to pray, meditate, sing your favorite hymn or HU, repeat a sacred phrase you cherish, or simply do the above exercise. Fill yourself with love before you begin. You can do this by thinking of someone or something you love and then letting the feeling of love take over as the images fall away. You are immersed in love!

Watch your life change from this very small discipline and others that help you remove your blocks to love. Fill yourself with gratitude that you have begun to make these changes with your loving efforts and the help of divine guidance.

You are loved so much, and each time you accept more of this love into your world, you expand and stretch your heart to receive even more each day. If *I* can do it, so can you, so keep on going!

How to Love Who You Are

KNOWING AND ACCEPTING WHO YOU ARE right now are the essential ingredients for loving yourself.

Who are you really? We have talked about the higher Self, the spark of God that is love, that is you. You are the Self. Right now you are living in a human form that is imperfect, that will always be imperfect, but is still miraculous.

Is it okay to accept our imperfections and love ourselves now while we strive toward an always higher state of being? Yes, it is. In fact, it is necessary in order to move forward spiritually.

"Helen" had an ongoing battle with herself. She kept telling herself that she would be worthy of love as soon as she had a new career and a new home and had lost forty pounds! She felt everything would be fine then and she would accept herself completely!

One day a friend told her about a special affirmation she wrote fifteen times a day until she felt more worthy. It goes like this:

I am a worthy vessel, a golden cup for the love of God.

Helen decided to try this exercise. Without counting she wrote, "I am a worthy vessel, a golden cup for the love of God." As she wrote, she sang the words and began to let those precious words into her heart. She began to realize that she was indeed worthy, and this insight brought her to tears. She released the feelings of unworthiness. She shed light on the dark places inside that said she was unworthy.

From this exercise, Helen came up with an acronym for the word *NOW*. It is No Obligation to Wait—No Obligation to Wait for that new career, new body, or new home. She intended to be worthy of God's love and her own love right now.

Helen's life has taken some dramatic turns, mostly in her attitude about life, her love for life, and her love for herself.

I decided to try this myself and realized that there always seems to be another step to take in feeling more and more worthy of God's love and in drinking in more and more of it every day while I expand my fuel tank!

Knowing and loving who you are is an ongoing process—at least it is for me. I hope it never stops, because that would mean I had stopped learning and growing, blossoming and expanding. How boring!

How can you more readily see the wonderful Self you are and love and respect that miraculous being? Here's another trick that I highly recommend you do first! I'm sure you will think of more.

Something You Can Do NOW:

In your journal, write a brief description of all the good things you know about who you are. Feel free to write anything—brag all you want—for no one needs to read this but you. Also, you can include the nice things others—such as family, friends, or business associates—may have said about you.

If you want help getting started, use the following list.

1. Write down your best qualities; your ideas about yourself; and positive comments about you from parents, siblings, friends, your mate or partner, business associates, and so on.

2. Write about how you help others and how you may affect others positively.

3. Write what you like to do for creativity and fun, and list your talents and skills.

Do you like who you are? If you do, that's great. What an important step to loving yourself! If you don't, maybe you can review some of those great qualities you have, or ask your very closest friends to tell you how great you are, in detail. Tell them it's a homework assignment you were given.

Write down what you like about what they said, and read it daily for thirty days (by then you will begin to believe it!).

LOVING WHO YOU ARE MEANS *BEING* WHO YOU ARE

What does it mean to "be who you are"? It's certainly a well-worn phrase that evokes a desire in many of us. I often wondered who I really was until I realized that the concept just means doing what I love and expressing myself in a way which fills me with happiness and joy.

Doing what I truly love, from the highest part of me, fills me with love. This has become a vital part of loving myself. I take time now to cultivate the fine art of telling myself the truth about what I really want. Like any truth, it is constantly teaching me new lessons.

A very interesting change occurs when we are completely honest about who we are in any moment. This happened, delightfully, to someone very dear to me. A friend of mine we'll call "Bernadine" was brought up in the era of the independent woman. She was a teenager in the '70s when women were beginning to realize they could have satisfying, fulfilling careers outside the home. This movement was such a strong social thrust, she found herself caught up in an assumed role. Bernadine simply moved through life assuming not only that she needed to support herself but also that she had to do it all by herself.

Her inner whisperings of home and hearth-keeping, gardening and decorating, even child-rearing, seemed to be out of step with the '70s woman. She even had longings of finding a man who would love her so much he would be delighted to support her (gasp!) financially and emotionally in these endeavors. Bernadine wanted to fill their home with love, which not only would be appreciated but also longed for by him as well.

Bernadine cast these whisperings aside as unstable dreams. After all, these images simply didn't fit with the image she had accepted as a daughter of the feminist movement. She was independent, strong, and disdainful of being supported by anyone else—let alone a man, for goodness' sake!

The years went by and Bernadine began to feel these longings more and more. She began to trust them and feel that maybe they *were* what was right for *her.*

When she finally came to terms with who she really was and what she really wanted, Bernadine had only to open her eyes to see that he was standing right in front of her! He was a dear friend who, until that time, had appeared as just exactly that, a dear friend only. Now she knew that he was the man she would marry.

As soon as she was able to tell herself the truth about what she wanted, she got it! And he's happy too, because it was exactly what he wanted as well. He loves her dearly and is delighted to have the woman of his dreams fill his home with light and love.

Bernadine can now fulfill her career of choice part-time as well as her hearth-keeping duties, which she loves. This is truly a modern fairy tale come true. Now that she's made one dream come true, she knows that there are many more options in life open to her, some of which she may have never dreamed possible. Now she knows that anything is possible. What about you?

Something You Can Do NOW:

To be honest with yourself about what you truly want, get out your journal and write the answers to these questions:

1. What makes you happy? What makes your heart sing?

2. What would you do with your life if you had millions of dollars and never had to work again, ever?

3. What makes you feel light and good and filled with love?

4. What have you always dreamed of doing but never done?

5. As you look at the answers to the above questions, choose one thing you would really love to do and decide now to look into it. You don't have to do it yet, just explore the feasibility. Let yourself play with it. Go to the library and find out everything you can about it.

Talk to people who may know about the subject, but be very quiet about this to anyone who knows you until you see some results. Well-meaning friends or family can "rain on your parade" with a comment or even just a look. I have no doubt you know just what I am talking about. It is hard enough to stay positive about our *own* lives, let alone someone else's.

❤ ❤ ❤

Writing down your goals and even setting dates for their attainment is a very powerful way of loving yourself. Just how powerful is writing goals? I will tell you that it has made my life work in ways I never believed possible.

There have been several studies done about writing. One study proved that the group of people who *wrote* their goals accomplished them one hundred to one over the group who simply thought about them and acted on them! Isn't that amazing? You have a hundred times greater chance of accomplishing what you want when you put it down on paper!

I believe it's because writing helps engage the imagination and create more thoughts and images in connection with the goal. It also feels to me that I'm making more of a commitment to it, on a subtle, subconscious level. The subconscious never sleeps, never judges, but carries out all of our thoughts and images. Holding an image that uses all of the senses—touch, taste, smell, sight, and hearing—creates a new program in your subconscious mind. Add this to your writing; you will move more surely toward your goal, and thus topple any roadblocks in the way.

So what do you *really* want out of life? Even if you can write down just one goal, put it away in a box or envelope and look at it in one year. You will be amazed at how much closer you have come to it. You may even have accomplished it. I challenge you to try this!

When I have done this myself, which is regularly, I'm always amazed at how magically things happen. I never know how they are going to be accomplished, but my goals come true in ways I could never have imagined. Respect who you are by respecting what you want, and then watch the miracles occur!

LOVING OR ACCEPTING YOUR PHYSICAL SELF IS PART OF LOVING WHO YOU ARE

Even though we are spiritual beings and so much more than our outward appearances, we often get caught up in human experience, understandably. It can be a real challenge to accept these physical bodies when we are surrounded by the illusion of perfection in the media and in movies. There are, however, ways to look at your physical self more lovingly.

Perhaps you don't like some part of your body because your culture says that it isn't beautiful. What if you lived in a different culture, where that quality was considered the most beautiful of all? If you could see yourself as loved ones see you, you would find they see the love in you first and foremost. Your physical self begins to become less and less of a focus.

Think about these two questions now for just a moment:

Can you see yourself as others see you? Can you see the beauty and love they see in you?

A gorgeous model who came to one of my workshops told me later than she never really liked her legs. One day she decided to appreciate her long, beautiful legs just as they were and to quit picking on herself and her imperfections! Yes, even models (*especially* models) are extremely hard on themselves. I'm often grateful I don't have to be under that intense self-scrutiny. What enormous pressure!

Do you find there are parts of your body you don't love and accept? Allow yourself to relax and open yourself to love, the most important key to appreciating your body temple. As we're told in Colossians (NRSV), "Above all, clothe yourselves with love, which binds everything together in perfect harmony."

Something You Can Do:

1. Every day when you look in the mirror and see "the enemy" (the part of your body you do not like), shift your focus and look for the beauty!

2. Pretend you are your own adoring mate. Look admiringly at yourself and tell yourself mentally all the things you like and love about your lover looking at you from the other side of the mirror.

   Remember that this person adores *all* of you. If that's hard to accept, think of the person you love most in all of life and ask yourself if you reject any part of that person's physical being. For example, women have adored their men's "love handles" even when the men thought these bodily features were disgusting, and men have loved women's full hips for all of time, even when *we* reject them.

3. Now begin to look inside yourself. See the love that radiates from the spiritual being you are. Accept that this is what others see when they look at you. Know that

your love is the most attractive quality you have and let it shine!

Something Else You Can Do:

While you're showering or bathing or when you're just lying in bed at night trying to relax and go to sleep (this works *great* for falling asleep!), do this exercise:

1. Tell all your body parts how much you love them and appreciate them. Tell them you are grateful for all they do for you every day.

2. Smile while you are doing this and really feel the love.

3. Start with your feet and go up to your head. Include all your organs too. Doesn't it feel great, as if you've just had a full-body massage?

LOVING WHO YOU ARE MEANS TRUSTING YOURSELF

Would you accept a relationship with someone you don't trust? Surely you trust those you love, and they trust you to do your best in life.

Does your relationship with yourself include that same trust?

Do you trust yourself as much as your family and friends trust you?

I don't think I ever realized how much other people trusted me when I was younger. I still have a difficult time thinking I've lived up to others' trust in me. I often felt a

HOW TO LOVE WHO YOU ARE   113

great burden of responsibility to validate the trust in me of loved ones, clients, or coworkers by doing perfectly what I felt was expected of me. When I felt I was somehow making a mistake that might affect someone else, I felt terrible.

Sometimes other people remind us to trust and be honest with ourselves in ways we cannot readily see.

For example, I was blessed to have a friend tell me what I needed to hear after making a move I was unsure of. I have made many moves to different parts of the country, and have felt inwardly guided by divine Spirit to do so. Some people are very stable in life and learn what they need right in one place, one job, and/or one family. Others need broader experiences on this earth, and evidently I am one of those people!

I realized one day, as my friends questioned my urge to move once again, that perhaps I was not doing the right thing. I began to doubt myself and no longer trusted my spiritual instincts as I always had. The entire time I lived in this new area of the country, I had absolutely no reason to feel it was right. Nothing told me it was right, and in fact my finances were in ruin after making this move. What could possibly be the divine reason for the move?

I found out later, on my way back to my previous home, that there were people in my church who had looked to me as a bridge. I liked everyone and was friends with everyone, but evidently there was a rift between two groups. Since I was only there six months, I had no idea there was any problem. Finally, when I left, someone told me what purpose I had served: Being friends with people from both sides of this wide river, I helped to heal this rift.

I will always feel blessed to have been of service in that way and to know that my spiritual instincts were still working!

Something You Can Do:

1. Think and write in your journal of a time you trusted yourself but thought you had made a grave error. Perhaps you still think you made a mistake back then. Did you learn anything from the experience? Would you have been able to learn the lesson without the experience?

2. Who was hardest on you—you or your friends, family, or coworkers?

3. How did the experience help you become more of who you are today? Do you consider yourself wiser, more mature, more loving toward others than you did then? Did that experience help you reach new heights in the ability to refrain from judging others?

4. Confirm to yourself now that no experience is ever wasted if you learn something from it. Very likely, others learn from it too. Masters of success tell us that anyone who has never made a mistake has never tried to do anything, especially anything worthwhile.

5. Try looking at an "error" that may still be bothering you right now. Ask yourself what your best friend would say about you in that instance?

❤ ❤ ❤

Loving who you are means knowing and trusting who you are, who you truly are. Even if you believe you are simply a human being, and that is all, you still deserve just as much love and respect as any other human being. If *God* loves you, why shouldn't you love yourself? Love who you are, because in all the world there is only one you and because, in some way, that *you* is a light to many, many people you see every day.

Chapter 8

Allowing Others to Love You

ALLOWING OTHERS TO LOVE YOU can be even more difficult than *giving* love. Giving love feels so good. It feels to me as if I am giving a gift and as if I've done something wonderful!

Why is it different than receiving love?

Receiving actually is a gift. It makes the giver feel special, as if they've done something wonderful!

Step by step, I've learned to accept more love from others in the form of compliments, hugs, gifts of time, and more. Asking for what we need is a good first step to allowing others to love us.

Can We Accept Help When It Comes ?

Can we ask for what we need, then accept it when it comes? I know this can be difficult, simple as it seems. I know that it *has* been for me. What I do now is just as I mentioned in being kind to yourself: ask how I would feel if I were my own best friend. Then I try to do what my best friend would advise me to do. I get the help I need, whether it is financial, physical, psychological, or spiritual. We need to first accept that we are not perfect and that we will always have the joy of giving help when it is requested and receiving help when we are humble enough to ask for it.

A good way to begin receiving help is to ask for it and accept it graciously. Very rarely will anyone refuse to help you when you need it or want it. Here's one very quick and easy way to begin.

HEALING THROUGH THE SIMPLICITY OF HUGS

One thing that struck me in the process of loving myself was that I was always giving hugs. That was very good, except that all I was doing was *giving*. I don't think I really *received* a hug until I was about thirty-five years old! I finally started to relax, feeling that the other person's hug was a gift from that person and from God. What a difference it made! Now I ask for hugs all the time. It feels so good to receive as well as give!

Maybe you are a master at receiving hugs. If you want to improve your huggability, try this next exercise.

Something You Can Do:

1. Think about your own answers to these questions: When were you last able to surrender to, receive, or

accept a hug *fully?* Did you ever exhale? Did you ever breathe into it? Or did you just feel as though *you* had to do the giving?

2. Try this the next time someone hugs you (or don't wait—*ask* for a hug!). If no one is there, hug yourself— it's great practice and shows you that you can indeed love yourself: *Just let yourself be hugged.* It sounds simple, doesn't it? Simple, but not necessarily easy.

Allow yourself to feel the hug, to breathe and relax in the arms of someone who cares about you. It's not that you should stand there limply with your arms hanging at your sides; you've got to hold on! Your viewpoint has simply changed from *giving* to *receiving* for a moment, which is what the other person really wants you to do or they wouldn't be giving you the hug in the first place!

You may want to tell the hugger what your goal is, so he or she understands the purpose. If you can get a hug a day like this for a while (and you don't *have* to hug back), you may find it very healing. You can trade off with your fellow hugger, but make sure each of you receives when it's your turn to receive.

3. If you think this is a burden for the hugger, think again! It makes *you* feel good to give to others, doesn't it? Well, that's how good it makes others feel to give to you! The only problem is that *someone has to be willing to receive.* By receiving a hug or anything else from a willing giver, you are actually giving back.

❤ ❤ ❤

I find that people who have trouble loving themselves are very often the same ones who have little trouble giving their entire lives to others. I discovered for myself that this was often because I really needed others to give me things such as attention, affection, respect—the things I lacked most of my life. Then I discovered how easy it was to get love, just by giving it to myself! The next step, of course, was learning to receive it, and I am certainly still learning all of the above.

LEARNING TO ACCEPT COMPLIMENTS

"Your hair looks great today!" Grace said to "Norma" as she waltzed into the workplace. Norma shuddered; "Oh, you've got to be kidding. You think it looks good? I couldn't do a thing with it this morning!"

After Norma's response to the compliment, how do you think Grace felt? Perhaps she felt embarrassed, put down, invalidated. What if Norma had responded to Grace's compliment with a simple "Thank you" and *nothing* more? Grace would have felt better. In accepting Grace's compliment with grace (no pun intended!), Norma could have made Grace feel good about herself, too, for giving the compliment. Beyond that, Norma may have realized that even on her worst hair days, her hair still looked good to others. Perhaps she would have recognized that her hair may look prettier because she *did* make a special effort, and someone noticed.

Think about how good you feel when you say something nice to someone and they begin to smile and glow and sparkle with the good feeling you are passing on to them. When they say, "Thank you; that makes me feel good," with sincerity, doesn't that kind of response make *you* feel warm and happy inside too? Now *two* people feel better!

Denis Waitley, the world-renowned trainer in the areas of success and self-esteem (author of *The Psychology of Winning*), instructs people to say "Thank you" in order to improve self-esteem when they receive compliments. After hearing him speak, I used Waitley's method. The instructions from him were something like this: "When someone gives you a compliment, say 'Thank you,' then shut up."

I found it difficult at first. Even so, I took his advice very seriously. Every time I received a compliment, I said "Thank you" as sincerely as I could, then *forced* my mouth closed and kept it that way until I could trust myself to speak. Over time it became easier to accept compliments this way. If I wanted to embellish a compliment, I could say something like "I'm glad you like it" or "That makes me feel very good." Such responses helped me feel that I was giving back when I needed to, but still graciously receiving their kind words.

After learning to do this, I found my life and attitude about myself changing dramatically. It forced me to accept others' complimentary views of me, thus sharing the views. The image of someone who actually looked or did something wonderful was not one I easily accepted about myself. Now I can accept more and more of it, not feeling as much need to "fish for compliments" by putting myself down.

Something You Can Do:

1. Think of whom you see often. Ask a friend or family member to compliment you as often as possible for just one week. Let him or her know you are willing to do the same in return next week.

2. The challenge: Request that he or she "call you on it" if you say anything to detract from the compliment. The person who gives the compliments is coach as well. Only positive statements about yourself or others are allowed.

    Examples: "Thank you!" "I'm happy that you like it," "That makes me feel great!" "I'll thank you for my hairdresser too."

3. Call your friend or partner right now and set this up.

ALLOWING OTHERS TO APPRECIATE YOU CAN BE LIBERATING AND JOYFUL FOR EVERYONE.

"Flowers for me?" Sarah could hardly believe it as she stared at the gorgeous array of roses and carnations that the delivery man held.

"You *are* Sarah Stone, aren't you?" he asked.

"Why, yes, that's my name." Sarah finally found her tongue in time to say "Thank you" as he handed her the unexpected, huge bouquet and hurried on to his next delivery. The flowers were from Michelle, a coworker for whom Sarah had pinch-hit the previous week during a family crisis. Sarah was stunned, but grateful. She was not used to such extravagance. She never really thought about how much her help may have meant to Michelle.

Sarah was used to helping out and not receiving much appreciation, so it almost felt uncomfortable to accept such an obviously expensive gift, just for being a friend. How could she feel more comfortable with it?

Sarah began to think about how much better Michelle feels now that she's let Sarah know how much she appreciated her help. Also, Michelle now feels that she can call upon Sarah again if need be, having given something in return.

WOULD PEOPLE LOVE YOU MORE IF YOU WERE PERFECT?

What if you met someone who was your idea of perfection? How would you feel about that person?

Would you like being around him/her?

Would you be able to relax and "be yourself"?

Do you really want to be "perfect," or do you want to be *happy*?

I realized one day that if I was going to truly be happy, I had to stop being so hard on myself and stop expecting myself to perform like a robot, doing every function perfectly.

If you are alive and living life to the fullest, errors are

bound to occur but so are wonderful lessons in living life better.

"Sally" was always feeling that she had "messed up." She was making mistakes right and left at work, and her personal relationships were far from smooth. What was she doing wrong?

One day a friend of hers said: "Do you think being perfect is possible? Would you learn anything if you were?"

Sally thought about these questions for weeks. The more she thought about them, the more she realized the reasons for her errors in judgment or in action. She was learning from them!

How else could she possibly learn life's lessons?

As Sally accepted this part of life more and more, that making mistakes was a natural occurrence to some degree, she began to accept *herself* more and more. Life became an adventure, a game to be played, with the love and joy of the activity, not the goal, being first.

As long as we are learning, nothing is ever really an error or a mistake. God loves us the way we are, our souls residing in imperfect, growing, learning forms.

WHAT IF SOMEONE SEEMS TO DISRESPECT YOU?

Other people may challenge our self-worth.

"Gina" had a friend who reminded her of her mother, a very critical woman, or so it seemed to Gina. We will call the older woman "Rose." Rose had a way of trying to control the situation by being "the expert" on every subject imaginable. It didn't matter what Gina was doing; Rose knew a better way to do it and would tell Gina so very clearly! "Gina," Rose would admonish, "why are you thinking like that? You should be thinking like *this*." Or Rose would say, "Gina, life doesn't work like that; life works like *this*." Gina knew Rose loved her, but felt unloved and hurt by Rose's blunt comments.

Rose always had the answers to questions that Gina had never even asked. Gina wondered about this. Surely, there was a lesson in all this. Gina tried to look at life from a spiritual perspective. This helped Gina see that a part of herself which she needed to look at more closely was being mirrored in Rose. Gina also knew that she could be very critical of herself, as well. She decided that Rose represented the "little girl" inside of her who needed attention.

So what could she do about it?

Gina used her imagination to envision this little child sitting on her own lap. She saw herself hugging the child and telling her that she loved her and would now give her the attention she needed. Then whenever Rose became critical and Gina felt reactive to it, she would stop herself from becoming defensive by picturing Rose as the little girl who needed attention. She would simply feel the love for Rose that she would feel for herself as the neglected-feeling child inside.

Amazing changes occurred from this experiment. Gina began to feel less and less defensive about Rose's comments. Rose began to be kinder with her comments or to keep them to herself altogether! Also, Rose was beginning to feel that changes were taking place within her as well, unknown to Gina. Rose woke up one morning when Gina was visiting and said: "I feel as if something is shifting in me. I wake up with backaches or headaches, but I know these are the results of good changes."

When Gina got ready to move away from the area where she lived, Rose gave her a hug and said, "Thank you for teaching me patience." Gina was awestruck. She had not intended to teach Rose anything or to change her in any way. All she wanted to do was to change and improve herself. This is how life works. When we control ourselves, the *situation* comes under control.

WHEN WE CHANGE OUR ATTITUDES AND TAKE RESPONSIBILITY FOR OUR OWN REALITIES, EVERYTHING AROUND US CHANGES.

Want to be in charge of your world and how it affects you? Try this next exercise and be ready for a greater awareness of your life and yourself.

Something You Can Do:

1. Pick a situation that causes a strong reaction in you— one which either angers or upsets you or causes fear, anxiety, or panic.

2. Write a brief paragraph about one particular incident. If you get stuck, write it as if you were a child explaining to a parent what happened, that is, "So-and-so did such and such to me."

3. Choose a phrase or word from the paragraph that clearly states or inspires the feeling you have as a reaction to the situation: for example, "He was overly critical" or "She completely ignores me."

4. Close your eyes for a moment to think about the following possibilities:
   - Does this phrase describe a part of yourself? (Do you criticize or ignore yourself?)
   - Does this phrase describe a person in your family, a childhood experience?

5. Now imagine that a part of yourself is doing this to you. Envision that part as a child desperately trying to get your attention. Try to hug that part of yourself. Give it unconditional love. Do this every day until you see a change in the situation. Each time you come up against a circumstance that seems hurtful or uncomfortable, look within yourself and give love to the part that feels the pain or discomfort, as if you were comforting a child who had been hurt or admonished. It is *that* simple. Love heals all. Watch the miracles occur!

❤ ❤ ❤

I used to have a difficult time accepting criticism from others. I felt that they were saying "I think you're stupid" or "I don't love you." Now I realize that people are usually more critical of themselves than they are of anyone else. Because I can now see this better, I can also accept more constructive criticism from those I love, knowing that it is usually coming from a loving, supportive place. Since learning to love myself more, I feel more certain that my life can be enhanced by others' sincere and loving observations, whether critical or complimentary.

Whether or not we know it, all of the experiences in our lives are there because of God's love for us. When someone is angry at me, there may be a lesson I need to learn that will wake me up to something important for me spiritually. On the other side of the same coin, that individual who is angry may be using me as a mirror for his or her own growth. The key for me has been to look for the love in every situation, no matter how far off it seems to be. It often takes a little time, after my initial human reaction, to find this love. Of course, I don't accept abuse of any kind; that's very different.

It also helps when *I* get miffed at someone and I don't understand why. Then I know that even though I feel bad about hurting someone's feelings, I also know that that person may have needed the experience—on some level that I will never know. *This is not an excuse to simply spew out anger or bad feelings!* We still need to be responsible for our feelings and actions. It's simply a way of looking at life from a broader view, especially when you have no idea why you have said something the way you have, or why it was received the way it was.

The assumption here is that all of the love in the world has the same source—God (or whatever your name is for God). If this is so, then all creation expresses love in one way or another, and I can receive this love by simply focusing on the love in others rather than the anger, criticism, or pain. When I am able to do this, I feel more love in my life.

It's easier to look at life and love this way when I fill myself with it daily. This is like exercising your spiritual muscles. Spiritual exercise is like physical exercise. It has to be done daily to be effective. (For more information about spiritual exercises, see "Suggested Reading" on page 215.) Whether you are most comfortable with prayer, meditation, or contemplation does not matter. What matters is visiting that wellspring of love, of life, daily. Since I have done that, I now expect more love from life, because I see how much there is each time I sit down to go within. I open my heart as much as I can, sometimes just thinking of how much I love my husband, my pets, or my friends, and it is amazing what a difference it makes in my whole day.

Of course, I may not remember to do this all the time, and I don't know whether *anyone* does. However, the more I put effort into seeing love all around me, giving and receiving it, the more joyful it is to be alive!

CHAPTER 9

Resolving Relationship Addiction

WHAT I THOUGHT OF AS "LOVE ADDICTION" haunted me for years until I found a way to tap into God's love in the simple things in life. Resolving a dependency on relationships was a process that went well with learning to love myself. The process helped me see that I really wanted the magical, unconditional love of God. When we're looking for that ideal in human love, are we not truly looking for God's love?

HEALING THE PAIN IN OUR HEARTS

For twenty years Greg had hung on to Michelle. She had drawn him in and then rejected him several times in succession. The torture he endured was unbearable at times, because he lived in the same apartment building as

Michelle during a time when they had freshly broken up and she was seeing another man.

Greg held a torch for Michelle for so long because he desperately needed love. He couldn't let go of even a shred of hope because it was right in front of him, so familiar. Would love ever come again?

The fear of being alone is so great in some of us. It makes sense that we grasp at straws when we're love-starved. I've been there, and I know what it's like to be so desperate for love that you hang on to anyone who's attractive to you, even when it's obvious to everyone else there is no hope whatsoever for a lasting relationship.

Having been starved for affection, touch, and even food when I was a baby, I learned to "milk" love from every situation possible, even if only in my imagination! In fact, I became very good at imagining someone loved me when he couldn't make even the most basic commitment of being on time for a date. My heart hurt all the time. I thought that was how *everyone* felt who was without a mate.

I felt terribly sorry for single people, because I thought they were all in this terrible pain that was such a pervasive aspect of my own life. Finally, I had to face the fact that my heart hurt because it needed mending. I was seeing my own pain reflected in everyone else.

I tried all kinds of therapy, which worked for short periods of time, but the pain would always come back. Finally, I went through a depression that lasted months. Any of my friends will tell you I had always been cheerful and energetic, so for me this was near death!

One day while taking a walk, I even hoped a truck would hit me. Luckily, I do not believe in giving up responsibility for my life through suicide, so I am here to tell you how I came out of that depression and how I got the pain in my heart to leave permanently.

Anyone can do what I did. I took the time for myself every day to do a special spiritual exercise to heal my heart. I used the ancient love song to God that I shared with you earlier—HU (pronounced *hue*, sung *Huuuuuuu-uuuuu*), which has been used for centuries by many different cultures and religions. You can use any prayer or sacred word or song that resonates with you. I then imagined a blue light, which gives a very soothing, healing feeling along with the sound of HU, flowing into my heart. I would take the time to lie down after work to do this exercise or would even do it during the day if I was going through a particularly painful time. When you lead a busy life, before falling asleep at night is another good time to do this.

It took many months to achieve results, but it was well worth it! My heart was finally healed, and since then, I have had no more of that constant ache in my chest. Since then, it only hurts on rare occasions if I feel sad about something, and even then it is only a gentle ache. Even then, I feel surrounded by a warm glow of love, as if someone were hugging me and I knew just who it was. It's God loving me through one of His wonderful messengers.

I must warn you that the above exercise to heal the heart is very powerful. Use this exercise as you feel comfortable, less or more often, for shorter or longer periods of time. For me it pulled up some very old, deep, and intense emotions, including anger, depression, and sadness. They had been buried for years. Get professional counseling or support in dealing with these issues if they feel overwhelming in any way.

WHAT HAPPENS WHEN YOU BEGIN TO HEAL?

As mentioned earlier, I had some warning when the anger was about to surface. During the day I would get irritated or frustrated about little things. Perhaps I would feel anxiety. If you do feel some of these things, you may want to get them out in a more controlled manner, after warning friends, coworkers, and family that you are in "surfacing mode."

Some ideas, as mentioned before, to release negative emotions safely are these:

- Scream in the car
- Tear up a newspaper
- Beat the kitchen sink with a dish towel
- Pound a pillow or the empty car seat beside you, or
- Get a nerf bat and beat on the wall or furniture.

Use your imagination for ways to release your anger or pent-up emotion that will be safe and not harmful to anyone or anything around you.

You may find yourself crying easily and releasing the emotion underneath the anger, which is often fear and pain of some kind. I find my anger giving way to tears almost immediately when I do the above "anger release" activities. Most important, it keeps me from venting that anger at some poor, unsuspecting clerk or loved one—which, believe me, has happened more than I care to think of. However, I did warn my friends that I was doing inner work and that I might be caught unprepared. I think I must have the greatest friends in the world! They were very understanding.

I highly recommend that you warn friends and loved ones if you try this and are serious about the results. It helps them know not to take things personally, especially if they are good mirrors for the issues you are working on! It seems my emotions came bubbling up to the surface in layers, like a layer cake of anger, sadness, fear, anger, sadness, fear, and so on. Everyone is different, so *your* experience will be unique. Look to the spiritual guidance in your life for help.

SUCCESS WITH THIS HEART-HEALING EXERCISE

Greg, whose twenty-year attachment is discussed earlier in this chapter, used this exercise with great results. He released the pain in his heart by doing the above exercise. Greg also had the "layer cake" effect. Then he got so strong and became so free that he was able to tell Michelle it was bye-bye time. After that, he felt even freer. Finally, Michelle was ready to make a commitment to Greg, because he was now committed to himself and she knew it.

Then we have "Cheryl," who thought relationships would never work for her. She had read every self-help book she could get her hands on and had finally let go of her then-current noncommitted partner. She used my heart-opening exercise with relish and got the "layer cake" treat too. Well, it's not exactly a treat, but it does make you feel better afterward! The good news is that her man was not only willing to commit to her after all this, but willing to work at the relationship as well.

As for me, it took longer than it took anyone else, including Greg and Cheryl. While I was healing my heart, I became involved with a man who was the least likely to commit of any of the men I had ever dated. He was a confirmed bachelor and had never been in love. He was perfectly content to live his life alone, and relationships were "nice, but not a priority," as he put it. He admitted candidly to never having grown up and never wanting to.

At the same time, he pursued me with flowers and sweetness, romantic dinners at expensive restaurants, theater and hand-holding, and walks along the river. He was always a gentleman and never sexist. He supported my goals and dreams in many ways, never giving unasked-for advice, and respecting my expertise in my field. I fell in love with his kind heart and decided that he had to be in love with *me* as well, or he would not have been treating me so wonderfully. Wrong! He was not capable of being in love, nor had he *ever* been.

When I finally began to realize that he may not have been in love with me (as I was with him), I tested my new-found inner peace and my newly strengthened heart. Even though it was scary for me to do this, I asked him what he really wanted. He said he did not know. I asked what his goals were for relationships. He said he did not know that, either. I asked if he ever wanted to get married (to anyone). Again, he didn't know.

Do You Deserve to Have What You Want?

I explained to him that we could only go so far together unless we had common goals. I told him I eventually wanted to be married—to the right person, of course. I asked him to take whatever time he needed to discover what he wanted and to call me when he knew, but not until then. That was very difficult for me to do, since I could have blindly gone along indefinitely enjoying his company. For the first time in my life, I was taking my life into my own hands and deciding that what I *really* wanted was okay!

He didn't call for two weeks. I weakened and called him. Did he know what he wanted? He said he thought he wanted what *I* did: In his heart of hearts, he wanted to be married to the right person. "Okay," I said, "I'll see you again."

I knew deep inside he was not being honest with himself, and therefore not with me. However, I gave him a second chance.

Within two weeks, he often seemed distant again, so I asked him once more. He said that he was thinking I wasn't right for him. To me this meant that marriage wasn't right for him, because he and I got along great. So I said, "Okay, I still want to be your friend, and we will enjoy each other's friendship, with nothing romantic—a platonic friendship only." I felt so free! I finally had the courage to *ask* for what I wanted. Now I was free to find someone who really *did* want to get married. However, this took some time.

Many men began to call me after that, and each one had a "gift" for me, a treasure chest of learning about what I really wanted. Never before had I allowed myself the luxury of saying "No" to people who simply weren't right for me in ways I would have ignored in the past because I had been so desperate for love.

After about a year of this, having great experiences meeting new men but still finding no "Mr. Right," I decided I was not even interested in dating. I had better things to do with my life than to examine and reject people, or to *be* examined and rejected! I had to go within once more and find out why I could not attract the person who was right for me.

The results of that time alone caused me to realize how much love was there, in my life, in the present moment. I learned to be in love with life itself. This helped me relax with the fact that I might have to live my life alone. It became easier to accept the possibility of never getting married again. I realized that I was happier alone than with someone who did not fit every description of my ideal mate.

If I was going to have a mate, he would have to be very, very special and he would have to be sent by God, since I had been unable to find him myself. I would proudly tell my friends, "He's going to have to knock on my door!"

Well, he practically *did* and we are now happily married! Not only that, but he is *more* than I ever dreamed possible.

The greatest gift in the world for all my heart-healing work is inner peace and a love so great that I feel lucky just to be alive. That love led me to my wonderful mate, who had been a friend for years. I just didn't have the eyes to see him for what he was for me, a lovely reflection of my higher Self and of God's love in my life. We're in harmony most of the time, and we both feel very lucky to have found each other. Even though we have our challenging moments, like any couple, it's so much easier than any relationship I've ever had. That's because I got the relationship with myself straightened out first!

One of the results of doing my heart-healing exercise was that I could see more clearly when people were not able to make a commitment in either personal or business relationships. I was able to let go of them more easily and was happier alone than with someone who wasn't right for me. That willingness to let go of something which was not right allowed me eventually to meet someone who *was* right. While I was alone for that year, I moved forward with joy, knowing I had a lot to give to life and a lot of love to share with whomever I could.

Would you like to try the exercise I did to heal and open the heart?

HEART-OPENING EXERCISE

In whatever way you commune with God daily, ask for help in opening your heart. Ask God to help you heal old wounds that keep love from being as fully present in your life as you'd like. Be willing to do whatever it takes, knowing it may take a lot of courage. Know that you have the courage and strength it takes through the support of the Holy Spirit, as you step forward into a new life. Of course you may make what you think are mistakes, but treat yourself gently and realize they are gifts from Life and move on. Trust yourself and your spiritual guidance to know exactly which steps you need to take. *Know* that God will bring you the tools you need to unlock the puzzle of your block to freedom.

Something You Can Do NOW AND DAILY:

1. Relax by lying down or sitting where you will be undisturbed for 20-30 minutes.

2. Take a few deep breaths, breathing into your heart area or anywhere in your body that you feel pain, fear, anxiety, sadness, loneliness, or other emotional discomfort. Focus your love and attention on whomever you look to for spiritual guidance.

3. Imagine a broad beam or large ball of blue light, which helps to heal the emotions, going into your chest.

4. Sing HU (*Huuuuuuu*), a love song to God, or any prayer or chant you wish.

5. Continue until you feel it's time to stop. Trust yourself to know.

During this exercise, you may feel yourself wanting to cry or write your feelings in your journal. You may even fall asleep. Let yourself do whatever comes to you. Notice over time how your attitudes change in relationships and how much more you rely on yourself to create the love in your life.

❤ ❤ ❤

Something Else You Can Do:

Say to yourself three times every day:

I am totally filled and satisfied by divine love. I now have more to give others.

In this exercise your focus shifts to giving, once you are filled. It changes the viewpoint from need to ability to give.

❤ ❤ ❤

Even in a wonderful, harmonious marriage there are times when people feel unloved. Words may fly in anger, or a loved one may need time alone. How can a mate handle that? There are many self-help books on communicating more clearly and lovingly with one's significant other. In order to be that calm and centered, listening with an open heart, I need to feel comfortable with myself, and I am sure most other people do too. When I feel the love that always surrounds me, then I can feel that calm comfort inside. Then I can listen lovingly, even when my mate is venting in a very dramatic way!

For me, remembering that the real, divine love is inside helps me not to be desperate for love and acceptance from others. The source of all love is readily available, and my husband simply reflects that love and gives it to me through his heart. If I am not feeling good about myself or worthy of love at that moment, he feels a "wall" and cannot give me what I think I need from him, unless I am clear enough to *ask* for it!

Any time I need love, however, I can always go directly to the source through any of the exercises I have shared in this book. After doing those exercises for years, now (when I remember!) I simply think of *being loved* and it comes more easily than ever before. That way, I am not dependent on any one person for the love I need in my life. *I* can take responsibility for being loved. I *think* I am loved, therefore I am!

BEYOND HEALING YOUR HEART

Being able to feel more love in my life has been such a challenge for me. I truly want to help others have an easier, more pleasant journey to love.

I found a way that worked for me to replace the romantic relationship I always felt I needed in my life in order to feel love. That way was to get a pet. For me it was a darling calico kitten that immediately bonded to me.

Even though she was almost a year old, she acted as though I were the only one she had ever known. I was in love with her immediately. When I came home, she scolded me with meows for being gone, and she woke me up each morning with kitty kisses of gentle bites and licks on my chin, purring all the while.

My cat was playful too and kept me in stitches much of the time. I don't recall any relationships with humans being quite that entertaining. I needed someone to love and someone to whom I could give. She filled that need for me. I learned from her that love can come from any-where and that I should expect it. I also learned that giv-ing love is getting it. The more I gave to her, the more I felt love, and in feeling it, I was getting it too!

Maybe you are unable to have a pet where you live. Consider voluteering with children, senior citizens, phys-ically challenged people or those who want to learn to read. Big Brothers and Big Sisters and other mentoring or-ganizations for youth have changed the lives of both the youths and the mentors. The love you give will always come back to you some time, some where, when you are ready to receive it.

GETTING WHAT YOU WANT

Giving yourself what you need is important. Finding a *healthy* way to do that is essential. When you're attracted to people because you need love and not because they are the kind of people you would want as good, intimate friends, step back for a moment. Ask yourself if there's an-other way to fill yourself and your life with love.

Think about what may be your mission in life and

your spiritual goals (see Appendix A "Exercises for Loving Yourself"). Finding what thrills you or makes you feel fulfilled is so important to having a life filled with love. If you are not sure what makes you happiest, take some time off to think about it. Isn't one day off work worth the happiness you will have for the rest of your life?

Spend some time doing exercises like the one following:

Something You Can Do:

1. Ask God for guidance to light up the highest and best in this exercise. Write down as many things as you can think of that you have ever wanted to do, just as if you were a child whose imagination knew no limits.

2. Now pick out the things which make you feel warm and good, which make you smile.

3. What can you do to begin to make them happen? Spend at least a few minutes a day doing something toward your dream. Read my booklet *How to Make Your Dreams Come True* if you are not sure where to begin.

If you've done all the Loving Yourself Exercises and still feel drawn to unhealthy relationships, unable to stop, *get professional help. You are worth it!*

Here is one more exercise to try for overcoming the addiction to human love. Do the following exercise every day for thirty days. See how different you feel at the end of the month.

Something You Can Do TO HEAL:

1. Breathe deeply and relax into your body. Invite your guardian angel or spiritual guide to be with you and guide you in this exercise daily.

2. Think of someone or something—such as a friend, child, or pet—that you love in some way other than romantic love. Say the word *love* to yourself and feel the love in your heart. Begin to sense the *feeling* of love for itself, letting go of any images of people or pets. Fill yourself with this feeling, as if it were a wonderful, glowing warmth.

3. Imagine that this feeling of love is pushing the pain, loneliness, or loss up and out of your body and dispersing it, like mist from a steaming pot.

4. Envision your angel or teacher with his/her hand on your heart, healing the old wound, smoothing the old scars, and making you whole. Imagine a white or golden light filling the area and feel the comfort it brings.

❤ ❤ ❤

The greatest gift I've ever been given has been the gift of divine love after healing my heart. There *is* no greater love. The love of another human is a very small reflection of the divine love that surrounds us always. If you find a way to experience that heavenly love, you will never settle for anything less than the highest love in your life now and always.

Wherever you go and whatever you do, you will never be lonely if you keep this love in your heart. Just ask for help with this and you will get it. Know that you deserve it, for it is your birthright. You exist because God loves you, because God loves, because God *is* love. God's love created life, and *you* are life too. You are as much God's child and an expression of God's love as anyone.

You are a special, precious soul, deserving of all the love life has to give. The next chapter will give you some ideas for manifesting more love in human relationships.

CHAPTER 10

Steps to Attracting the Right Relationship

AS YOU LEARN TO LOVE YOURSELF MORE, better relationships will automatically enter your life. However, it never hurts to give them a little help! This chapter gives you a step-by-step approach to bringing the right romantic relationship to you for this time in your life. If you are ready for a lifetime commitment, these steps can help you get *there* as well.

I've seen myself and many others go through some very definite steps in creating relationships that are beautiful reflections of divine love in their lives. If you have this desire, you may feel buoyed by the stories and exercises to come.

BUILD ON SOLID FOUNDATIONS

Three important foundations for a lifetime of love are these:

1. Having the right relationship with yourself, which begins with knowing your connection with God and living from that divine love within you.

2. Being willing to believe you can have the right relationship with others.

3. Expanding yourself to accept greater and greater amounts of love.

I honestly believe with all my heart that *if you feel filled with love and surrounded by love, you will attract love.* The love overflowing from you touches others in a magical way. This is the only key you may ever need to find the love you seek. The love of God in your heart makes all things look beautiful and makes it easier to return the love that you attract. This happens even with those to whom you had never before felt attracted.

A perfect example of this is when I finally noticed how attractive my friend was becoming. He and I had worked together briefly eight years before and had gone out together as friends (or so I thought). He had more in mind than just friendship, but I simply didn't see it. He was too shy to say anything, so *he* wasn't ready, either.

One day, eight years later, we met again at a seminar far from both of our homes, which were in different states. I knew almost immediately that he was right for me, and he is. He is my husband today. If I had not learned to carry the divine love in my heart, knowing it would attract the highest and best relationship for me, I don't think I could have seen this man for who he is.

This is a story you may have heard several times before—an old friend becoming a mate! Look for gold in the most unlikely places and trust your love-filled heart to know what is right for you.

Accepting greater and greater amounts of love may simply be a matter of practicing opening your heart to receiving. If you have been doing the Loving Yourself Exercises and giving more love to yourself, you are already practicing receiving more love. From doing these exercises over time, your heart will automatically expand.

"IMAGINATION IS MORE IMPORTANT THAN KNOWLEDGE."

One key principle in achieving success is imagination, our divine gift. Albert Einstein said, "Imagination is more important than knowledge." This, from a genius! Ask people who have been successful how they started, and nine times out of ten, I'll wager, they began with a dream, an image of some splendid road upon which they were about to travel. They only found out later how much work it would entail! However, the work was a labor of love, motivated by the golden dream. The image beckoned on butterfly wings, keeping the dreamer moving ahead with conviction.

So how does one apply imagination to attracting the right relationship? Read on and follow the road map to create your own adventure-filled journey to a loving relationship.

With the foundations of honoring your true Self, believing, and accepting more love in your life, the following steps will work well for you. Follow them to create a loving relationship that is the highest and best it can be for you. Remember that the subconscious plays a central role in our lives and responds to thoughts, feelings, senses, and images.

STEP ONE: DECIDE WHAT YOU REALLY WANT IN A MATE

In order to find someone who has the qualities you desire, of course, you must know what those qualities are. Perhaps you envision a kind, caring person. Later you think about communication, then fun and playfulness. Think about what's most important to you.

Write down every single quality you desire in a mate. There is no limit. I wrote 156 on my list!

Would you like someone who has a good sense of humor? How about honesty about oneself, good communication skills, or healthy self-esteem? Whatever qualities you want, these are the qualities *you* must also have. Developing those qualities opens the space for him/her to come along. Decide whether you treat yourself the way you expect your loved one to treat you. If not—well, get on it!

As stated, the right relationship begins inside, of course, with the relationship with yourself. That has been covered in the other chapters of this book in relation to self-commitment, self-acceptance, receiving love, and so on. The commitment to yourself includes doing what you love and knowing what makes you happy. In this way, you will attract a healthy, balanced mate like yourself. Then your relationship will begin on much healthier ground.

STEP TWO: CREATE A KEY IMAGE

What I call a "key image" is a specific scene, taken from your perfect fantasy for your ideal mate. To develop a key image, think of a scene that fits your image of the right relationship. Here is an example:

Key Image: A toast at your twenty-fifth wedding anniversary party.

I liked using the above key image before I met my husband, because I wanted a lifelong marriage and realized I would have to do better than just imagining myself getting married. I'd done that once already, and it hadn't lasted long. I wanted to *stay* married. Think about what you want and how long you want it to last, then make your key image fit your goal.

IMPORTANT: The people in your image are faceless. You are the only one you know. Putting someone else in the picture would be interfering with someone else's life, because your thoughts are powerful and can influence someone else unknowingly. Do not include anyone specific other than yourself in your creations. (Also, Spirit knows more about what is truly best for you—believe me, I know this from firsthand experience!) Just as *you* want and deserve the freedom to create and control your own life, so do others. It is your divine right and theirs as well. Be very careful with this. Enough said. On to the fun stuff!

Get out a recipe card or lovely piece of stationery and write "Key Image for an Ideal Mate" on the top, as if it were your recipe for success. As in the example to follow, use the first-person form, that is, "I am" statements, and all of your senses and feelings to bring the key image right into the present moment so that your subconscious believes it's real. This is how successful people create what they want in life!

Here's how your key image might look on paper:

I am lifting my glass to toast my husband at our twenty-fifth wedding anniversary party. He's smiling at me warmly and lovingly, as usual, with that wonderful twinkle in his eye! I can tell he still thinks the sun rises and sets in me. How wonderful it feels to be this loved! Now I am aware of the friends surrounding us. There's even more love to share. I hear the glasses tinkling as everyone toasts us. I smell the wonderful cologne my husband wears just for me. I taste the cake my best friend so lovingly made for us. It is the same type of cake we had at our wedding twenty five years ago—still my favorite! Now my husband is taking me in his arms and dancing with me as if we were teenagers.

The feeling of being "best friends" forever is only a shadow of how close we truly feel to each other after many years of working together to build a good life, love, and superior communication. Laughter in the air tonight is abundant, as it always has been in our life together.

This is the best night of my life—I'm as happy as I was when we got married! Life just keeps getting better, even though it doesn't seem possible. Our love is stronger, surer, and sweeter than ever before. I feel more grateful than words can say.

Read and focus with feeling on your key image daily for at least thirty days. Do this when you are most relaxed. The subconscious is most open and receptive upon awakening or just before falling asleep. Utilize that time to its fullest to commune with God, yourself, and your special dreams.

Try to become childlike. Children have no qualms about using imagination. It's as natural as breathing to them. As a child, it's okay to pretend or make believe. Why should kids have all the fun? Use all the positive childlike qualities you can muster; pretend you're now exactly how and where you want to be, and *believe it.* Eventually, if you keep pretending, you will be there.

Whatever You Focus on Is What You Receive

"Stephen" decided he wanted to get married, so he looked around and noticed that his house was too small. He began to make plans to remodel and expand it, making room for a wife and perhaps their first child. Next, he went to a video-dating service, described himself honestly, and met—*no one!*

A few months later he met a woman while working on a project on which she had volunteered to help. She became a good friend and they got along famously, talking for hours over the phone. Since he did not sense any romantic interest on her part, he maintained his viewpoint of her as a friend. Once she realized that he was exactly what she wanted in a mate and told him so, they began dating and got married a few months later!

Stephen had focused on what he wanted, and he was relaxed about the outcome. He and his wife both worked to be the best they could be, inside and out, and they both feel very lucky to have each other.

People who have succeeded in anything will tell you that they worked at it and that they also started with a dream. Walt Disney had one of the most childlike imaginations, and his company has become one of the biggest in the world. Conrad Hilton dreamt about owning his own hotel one day. The Hilton hotel chain is now one of the largest in the world. Gold-medal winners will tell you that they never even dreamed about losing. Winning was the only thing they could imagine.

This is how powerful focused imagination can be—and it works in love, as well as in business. Use it. It's your divine gift. Just be sure you keep yourself balanced after each image by saying, "Thy will be done," and you will be happy with the results in your life. In this way, you can "let go and let God," knowing the outcome will be *better* than you may have imagined.

Something that works really well for me if I am unhappy or lonely is to *imagine* myself being happy and fulfilled. I may envision myself feeling good within the next few days or even the next few hours, depending upon what I am working through. I try to muster an inner snapshot of myself being content, no matter what. It works every time, even if it takes a tad longer than projected. This is a very attractive state to be in! People love to be around others who are happy, content, fulfilled, and cheerful about life.

Now here is the secret, and this is important: I do not think about *how* I got there (to the happy state)! It's of no consequence whatsoever. The *how* takes care of itself when you focus on the goal. The subconscious mind is very powerful and so is Spirit. The answers come when you imagine they will. You don't have to know how everything works in order for it to work. You know how to drive a car, but you may not know all the mechanics or how steering or shifting gears works—you just drive!

Also, when I respect the thought "Thy will be done" instead of "my will," I find life to be much easier to understand, and it moves along more smoothly too. Notice the operative word here is *when*. Oh yes, I'm still working on this one, and probably always will be!

So even though we can't control other people, we *can* control ourselves and eventually how we feel. This can be done quite gracefully when we use our God-given gift of imagination.

Does it seem too simple?

Aren't the very best things in life simple?

It may not always be easy, but it *is* simple.

STEP THREE: BE GRATEFUL

Another step to relationship success is being grateful. When I've been grateful for any amount of love in my life, even though it seemed very little at the time, I always got more. It was truly miraculous. When I moaned about what I didn't have—whether to myself, my friends, or to God—I would find what I *did* have was diminishing! I decided to work on being grateful even more.

Being grateful works to keep us on top of life because it helps us stay focused on the positive. Whatever we focus upon is what we receive, so a focus on lack creates more lack. I wanted to keep the good things going in my life, so I worked on that.

When I was single, wanting very badly to have a companion with whom to share my life, I decided that I should be grateful for the freedom I had as a single person. I tried to think of all the things that made being single fun and carefree—like leaving a party whenever I felt like it, eating chips and salsa in bed, running out to see a silly movie on a whim, and many other crazy things which may take a bit more planning when married.

Now I am married to someone who makes me feel just as free as when I was single and would happily eat chips and salsa in bed with me if I wanted. I truly believe my good fortune now is because of my being grateful for my freedom when I had it! I enjoyed it as much as I could and did not try to "push it away" mentally. If I had, perhaps I would have attracted a mate who took my freedom as well!

Something You Can Do NOW:

1. Think of the love you have right now in your life—from parents, children, a mate, pets, friends, family, classmates, church mates, coworkers. Sometimes a smile from a stranger can bring more love than from anyone you know.

2. No matter how small the amount of love, even from small compliments or courtesies, gather all of it in your mind. Then let it flow into your heart. Feel the warmth and joy of it.

3. Now imagine surrounding yourself with this love. Thank God or your own higher power for all the love in your life. Feel thankful that you have the love you have, from wherever it comes.

STEP FOUR: PRETEND YOU ARE IN LOVE

The next step is to pretend that you're already in love with someone right now. Not just anyone—this person is the love of your life. It's someone who adores you for who you are right now, this very moment. It's like having an imaginary friend. It's embarrassing to admit, but I used to love having an empty seat next to me at the theater so I could pretend my husband was sitting next to me. The first time I went to a play with my husband I told him about my fantasy, and of course, he understood completely.

When I reached the stage of pretending I was in love already (before I had even *met* my husband), people would ask me if I was in love, because, they said, "You have that glow about you!" I really *felt* it too! It made me feel happy and fulfilled, as if there really was someone in love with me too—I just didn't know who he was! This helped me believe he was coming and accept his love when he finally did arrive.

I remember when I was younger feeling as though it would never happen, *could* never happen. Then when I did finally fall in love, I would think, "This can't really be happening to me; it feels too good to be true." So, of course, it went away. Until we can spiritually, mentally, and emotionally accept a solid, healthy, steadfast love, it will never stay.

Imagining you are in love will help it stick when it does come, because you will have gotten used to the feeling. Practice this feeling of being in love as much as you can and see how happy it makes you feel.

WRITE LOVE LETTERS TO YOUR IMAGINARY LOVER

For the brave and bold: Write a letter to your imaginary sweetie as often as you like in your journal or on special stationery. You can even save it until the real sweetie arrives. In the letter you could tell him or her what you did today, how glad you are to have him or her as your closest friend, and so on. Use your imagination. You could even plan trips or outings. Don't be surprised if later on you find yourself doing the exact things you've planned. Be patient and never give up. If you truly want someone special, it may take time to ready yourself. I know I certainly needed all the time I had!

PLAN YOUR WEDDING

Does planning an imaginary wedding sound crazy? Well, I thought I was crazy, but I did it anyway. It was fun. If you are a woman, planning a wedding is in your blood. I thought I was a "New Age woman," beyond the petty details of wedding dresses and flowers, but I realized that was a big part of why I wanted to get married! It's like being a princess for a day. When I planned my wedding, I just knew that I would be getting married someday soon—and just one year later, I did!

"Acting as if" something is going to happen can make it happen.

Take this as far as you feel comfortable. I planned every detail of my wedding and enjoyed every minute of it. I looked for and purchased my dream wedding dress (check out resale shops and rental options too, if you're on a budget), planned the menu including my favorite cake, and even chose a beautiful location right on a river, with catering facilities. When sales clerks asked me when I was getting married, I said "November" without batting an eye. I didn't say which November, and I simply allowed others to assume whatever they would. There was no need to explain what I was doing; after all, I *was* the customer!

Now guess when I got married. That's right, November! Of course, I went over all my plans with my then-fiancé before our wedding, and he felt very good about them all. We really were in harmony, and this proved it to me even more. When he saw me in my wedding dress, I knew that he was feeling so many things at once. The look in his eyes returned all of the love, patience, and effort I had put into the wedding and into creating this wonderful experience.

I had so much fun planning the wedding, I almost felt that I had fulfilled a special desire. It had been a great joy. Also, I thought, *Now, when we meet and decide to marry, I can just enjoy the engagement without all the time and stress of planning.* What a joy it was to be free and do what I wanted with my life!

If *I* can do this, so can you! We are no different, you and I, just parts of the same wonderful Spirit that is here just waiting for us to receive Its magnificent gifts.

STEP FIVE: TAKE ACTION

If you haven't already done everything you can think of to meet a kindred soul, why not have fun exploring the possibilities? Clubs and organizations, hobby classes, spiritual-growth seminars, dating services, volunteer work, and many other options exist for your discovery.

I found that a very discreet video-dating service helped me explore myself better than anything else. I learned what I really wanted in a mate, as well as what I could not accept and what I was willing to negotiate. There's no substitute for good experience! Even though I didn't meet my husband that way, I met myself and I realized eventually what I felt most comfortable with.

STEP SIX: LET GO AND SURRENDER THE OUTCOME TO GOD

The very last step is letting go and letting God take over. I had to be willing to face my greatest fear—being alone the rest of my life. Once I could finally face it, it wasn't so bad. After all, who wants to be with someone just to be *with* someone? If it wasn't the right person, it would not be fun. I'd already done that, so no need to go backward. I had a lot going for me, personally and spiritually. I decided I would enjoy the adventure of life and of service to my fellow human beings in my work as an author and in other endeavors. Life became more satisfying, and I continued to be grateful, filling myself with love daily.

The happy ending did come for me—or should I say, the happy beginning? Of course, my husband and I are constantly working to understand each other better and become closer friends. We are human beings, so our relationship can only be as perfect as we are (not!).

When you are creating your ideal relationship, remember to look forward with a positive attitude to the growing experiences you will have. The more love I can give to my husband when he's having a bad day, the more understanding he will be with me when I'm not at my best.

We laugh with each other about our stubbornness and many other idiosyncrasies. That keeps our perspective focused on what's really important—our love for each other.

If you use all the steps involving decision, creation, action, and release, you will attract the right relationship for you at this time in your life, for the lessons and experiences you need. When the time is perfect for you to be in love, you *will* be.

Exercises for Loving Yourself

REMEMBER THE OLD SAYING about charity beginning at home? That saying really means that love begins inside— within yourself, within your heart.

The following exercises are meant to be used whenever you need to fill yourself with love so you have more to give. Loving Yourself Exercises from previous chapters, plus some additional activities, are grouped for quick, easy reference or for review after you have already read the body of the book.

You may want to use exercises for specific occasions or to add them to your repertoire for speed in overcoming blocks to love. Use just one of these a day for a little while, such as one week, and watch the results! You'll find your heart opening more to yourself and to others around you.

Muscles don't strengthen unless we exercise them. In fact, they *lose* strength if we don't use them. Think of these exercises as strengthening and stretching your capacity for love, both in giving and receiving.

Something You Can Do TO BEGIN:

1. Find a quiet time, about a half hour, to relax all by yourself (even if you have to lock the bathroom door and take a bath to do it!).

2. Relax your body, and breathe deeply. As you exhale, release all tension, starting with your feet and working up to your head. Imagine clouds floating through your body—skies of blue calming and infusing your entire being. In your mind, go to your favorite spot to "get away from it all."

3. Now you are in touch with your higher Self. Think of all the love you have ever given and received. Ask this question of your higher Self: "How will it serve the highest purpose for me to love myself more?"

4. Write your answer here or in your personal journal.

_____

_____

_____

_____

_____

_____

_____

_____

_____

_____

_____

_____

5. Ask how life will be when you are filled with love that springs completely from within you. Write your answer here or in your personal journal.

_____

_____

_____

_____

_____

_____

_____

_____

_____

_____

Something Else You Can Do to begin:

Think of someone you know who has a lot of self-confidence and seems to have plenty of love and respect for him or herself. Try to catch the feeling that you think that person may have inside. That feeling could be confidence, calmness, or ease with others. See if you can capture this feeling every night before you go to sleep and every day upon awakening. It might help to repeat to yourself as you are falling asleep or anytime at all, "I feel completely and totally loved for exactly who I am at this very moment."

LOVING YOURSELF EXERCISES FOR YOUR PHYSICAL SELF

Loving Your Body Exercise
1—SELF-MASSAGE

Give yourself a face, foot, or scalp massage, especially when you are feeling tired or tense. It's one way of thanking your body for all the hard work it does for you. It's also a way of giving your body the love it needs.

If you can afford to do it, schedule weekly or monthly massages from a professional massage therapist. You may also call a massage school to see if any students need people to practice on (and it may be free!).

Loving Your Body Exercise
2—RITUAL BATH

Take healing mineral or bubble baths by candlelight. Set up a ritual time for them, such as Friday evening after a week's work. To make this a really relaxing experience, you can get bath "pillows" from department stores for under $5. While relaxing in the tub, imagine you have stepped into the healing waters of life, which in reality are pure love. Imagine that you are surrounded by this love every time you bathe or shower. You can even imagine drinking in love every time you drink water.

Loving Your Body Exercise
3—AEROBICS

Set up a regular schedule for physical, sustained aerobic exercise such as brisk walking, swimming, dancing, cycling, and so on, under a doctor's supervision if you have any health concerns. This is a great treat for your body and a mood lifter every time! Ask yourself if your health and happiness are worth three hours a week or so. One exercise expert stated that if the benefits of exercise could be bottled and sold over the counter, someone would make millions. Notice how much better you feel and how much *more* you are able to get done due to this increased energy level.

Loving Your Body Exercise
4—FOOD ENHANCEMENT

What you eat can reveal how much you are loving yourself. Many foods and drinks contain harmful substances that affect us negatively. Take a look at what foods are in your refrigerator and cupboards. Read the list of ingredients. Are the foods filled with preservatives, sugars, and chemicals or fillers? If so, be patient in making changes. Simply see if you can gradually add more healthful foods to your meals to shift the balance. New foods or beverages may add health or energy that you need to feel tops. This may mean taking time to do more food preparation for yourself, even if you cook just for yourself. I found I felt much better when preparing fresh food for myself.

Loving Your Body Exercise
5—SELF-ADMIRATION

Every day when you look in the mirror and see "the enemy" (the body you don't like yet), shift your focus and look for the beauty! Pretend you are your ideal mate. Look admiringly at yourself and tell yourself mentally all the things you like and love about your lover looking at you from the other side of the glass (mirror). Remember that this person adores *all* of you. If that's hard to accept, think of the person you love most and ask yourself if you reject any part of their physical being. For example, women have adored their men's "love handles," even when the men thought these bodily features were less than lovable.

Loving Your Body Exercise
6—SELF-APPRECIATION

While you're showering or bathing or when you're just lying in bed at night trying to relax and go to sleep (this works *great* for falling asleep!), do this exercise:

1. Tell each of your body parts how much you love them and appreciate them. Tell them you are grateful for all they do for you every day.

2. Smile while you are doing this and really feel the love.

3. Start with your feet and go up to your head. Include all your organs too. Doesn't it feel great, as if you have just had a full-body massage?

LOVING YOURSELF EXERCISES FOR YOUR
EMOTIONAL SELF

Loving Your Emotional-Self Exercise
1—BEING IN LOVE WITH LIFE

1. Think about how you would feel if you truly loved
   everything about yourself and your life. How do you
   think you would treat others? Would you be serving
   others rather than expecting to *be* served? Would you
   be complimenting people more and criticizing less?
   Would you feel that you were on a more equal basis
   rather than superior to others?

2. Try to imagine how wonderful it would feel to be in
   love with life, and write your insights from that perspective.

_____

_____

_____

_____

_____

_____

_____

_____

_____

_____

_____

Loving Your Emotional-Self Exercise
2—PRINCE/PRINCESS CHARMING

Using all of your senses, imagine this as clearly as you can:

Your very own Prince/Princess Charming rides up to you on a magnificent white horse. She/he is dressed in much finery and is obviously feeling very comfortable in the finest clothes. Looking fit and healthy, she/he is relaxed and calm. A quiet self-confidence exudes from every pore.

She/he is emotionally stable and balanced, feeling and expressing all that is within his/her heart—kindness; pure, unconditional love; and truth. She/he has no hidden anger or fear, only love. She/he knows exactly what she/he wants and is willing to do anything to obtain it. There is a very open heart residing within him/her, and it speaks of a love so rare that it can only come from one place—heaven itself.

Let this feeling of love surround you and linger as you go about your day. There is no harm in imagining yourself surrounded by love, as long as you don't expect it from any particular source. In fact, it can only bring more love to you.

Loving Your Emotional-Self Exercise
3—GIFTING YOURSELF

1. Think of something you have been wanting someone to buy you for your birthday or a holiday or perhaps just because you want someone to care enough to no-

tice that you want or need it. (Fill in the blank or write in your journal.)

_____

_____

_____

_____

_____

_____

_____

_____

_____

_____

2. Make a commitment to yourself RIGHT NOW to get this item for yourself. Sign and date this like a contract here or in your journal.

_____date_____

No excuses! If you don't have the money right now, you can:

   a. Save $2 a week in a specially marked envelope and place the money in a drawer.
   b. Go to a secondhand store or thrift shop and look for the item.
   c. Do some extra work or look at what you might sell to get it.
   d. Imagine you are buying it now. Do a visualization/imagination exercise to reprogram your subconscious just like a computer.

Loving Your Emotional-Self Exercise
4—FOUNTAIN OF LOVE

Sit quietly and take a few deep breaths. Each time you breathe out, let all the tension in your body flow out. Imagine walking through a vast, lonely desert. Feel the sand shifting under your feet as the sun's warmth penetrates your clothing. The only sound is the wind, which only adds to your throat's dry, parched feeling. It seems you're the only soul for miles upon miles. A green speck appears in front of you. It could be an oasis. You become hopeful and continue to move in the direction of the bright green area in the distance. You get close enough to see that it is indeed an oasis. As you get much closer to it, you hear the most beautiful melody on earth coming from its center.

Now imagine yourself walking into this oasis. You're struck by the beauty of the lovely white-marble fountain in its center. Next to the fountain stands your guardian angel. Filled with love, light, and the music of heaven, she/he offers you a golden cup filled with liquid from this fountain. You accept it gratefully. The water is sweet and pure, more refreshing than anything you've ever drunk. You feel its magical quality filling you with the most sublime, unconditional love you have ever felt. Your angel then invites you to step into the fountain. You do so and feel completely surrounded by this love.

Know here and now that this is God's love for you and that this feeling can be gotten directly at any moment in time simply by opening your heart to it and allowing it to encompass you like a warm hug. Imagine that this is happening now.

Loving Your Emotional-Self Exercise
5—HEART HEALING

1. Every day after work or before sleeping, breathe deeply a few times and relax. Pay attention to the sound of your breath and it will relax you.

   Now think of where you feel emotional pain in your body. Is it in your chest? Your stomach? Your head? Wherever it is, imagine filling that area with blue light, which is calming and healing for the emotions.

   In addition, you can use a holy word that is dear to you or the sound of HU, an ancient love song to God. It's pronounced like the word *hue* and sung in a long, drawn-out breath (*Huuuuuuuu*). It can be found in many different cultures and religions (the word *hallelujah* was derived from HU) and can be heard in sounds of life all around us. If you prefer, sing "Hallelujah" or any spiritual phrase that you feel is powerful and comforting for you. You can speak or sing silently to yourself or out loud. Or just think of the most beautiful, uplifting music you can imagine.

2. As you fill this area of pain within you with light and sound, add love to it. Feel the love you have for the little child you were who got hurt. Feel God's love for you healing the old wounds.

   WHAT TO EXPECT: If you do this exercise regularly, you may be surprised by some of the wonderful consequences. But first, you may feel some emotions needing to be cleansed. Emotions are normally felt and then released. However, if there is trauma associated with those emotions, then the emotions are suppressed until we are fully able to experience them, which is how they are released.

Unfortunately, emotions can be released at the most embarrassing times, when we're totally unprepared. A button has been pushed inside us, but we often don't even realize it until it's too late and the damage has been done. Most good therapists use methods to get us to feel things we don't want to feel, and that can be good if it's really necessary. Then we can release those emotions safely and create more space for love. We often need help in dealing with very difficult emotions, so I encourage you to seek professional counseling if these emotions come up intensely and repeatedly without relief.

Loving Your Emotional-Self Exercise
6—TIME FOR YOURSELF

If you have been feeling rushed, pressured, stressed, and generally ready for membership in the rat race, do the unthinkable—set aside separate, special time just for yourself, with absolutely nothing planned! If you have an appointment calendar (if you don't, that's one reason you are stressed!), get it now. Set aside one whole afternoon every week or as many weeks as possible, in the month. I know you can find at least one.

Write in big letters "R&R." In military language, that's "Rest and Recreation." You can choose either one, but make sure it is absolutely, positively *not* related to anything that sounds, tastes, or smells like work. I have found the best way for me to do this is to plan absolutely nothing and do whatever my little heart desires. In today's fast-paced, high-stressed world, doing nothing is an art many of us sorely need to cultivate.

If you have difficulty planning time for yourself, start small and sneak up on it! Whenever there's an unexpected opening in your schedule (a cancellation of an appointment, for example), use the opportunity to do something you'd enjoy, rather than automatically filling the time with more work (unless, of course, you are *at* work!). This will help you get the hang of it, and it will be easier for you to actually plan time for yourself in the future.

Loving Your Emotional-Self Exercise
7—LOVING WHO YOU ARE

Write a brief description of all the good things you know about who you are in your journal or here. Feel free to write anything—brag all you want—for no one needs to read this but you. Also, you can include the nice things others—such as family, friends, or business associates—may have said about you. Use the following list to help you get started.

1. Your best qualities (your ideas and those of your parents, siblings, friends, mate, and so on.

_____

_____

_____

_____

_____

_____
_____
_____
_____
_____
_____
_____

2. How you help others, how you may affect others positively.

_____
_____
_____
_____
_____
_____
_____
_____
_____

3. What you like to do for creativity and fun, your talents and skills.

_____
_____
_____
_____
_____
_____

_____

_____

_____

Do you like who you are? If you do, that's great! What an important step to loving yourself! If there are parts of yourself you don't like, maybe you can review some of those great qualities you have or ask your very closest friends to tell you how great you are, in detail. Tell them it's a homework assignment. Write down what they say, and read it daily for thirty days. By then you will begin to believe it!

_____

_____

_____

_____

_____

_____

_____

_____

_____

_____

_____

Loving Your Emotional-Self Exercise
8—LOVING THOUGHTS

Write here or in your journal the following:

1. Thoughts you have about yourself that are limiting, hurtful, invalidating, or negative in any possible way,

such as "I'm too fat" or "I'm not lovable." When you make a mistake, drop or spill something, do you tell yourself you are stupid, or something of the sort? It's very common, so don't be hard on yourself! Just be aware of it so you'll be able to change it.

_____

_____

_____

_____

_____

_____

_____

_____

_____

_____

2. Read them over as if they were written to you by a good friend.

3. Ask yourself these questions: "If my friend really said all of those things to me, would I continue to spend time with that person?" "Would I continue to be friends with him or her?"

4. The next time you have one of those thoughts, view it as if a friend had said it. You are your own best friend. Change the negative or limiting thought to a positive, loving one. Love yourself as you love your neighbor.

Loving Your Emotional-Self Exercise
9—TAKING CONTROL

When feeling sorry for yourself, you can imagine your way out! No need to continue to feel like a victim. Get out your journal and begin to write:

1. Choose a situation in which you find yourself often feeling rejected, lonely, criticized, unloved, or challenged in some similar way. Write the story with all the feeling you can muster. Really dramatize it. Some of those feelings come from a very deep place and are perfectly valid. (If it feels out of hand, definitely see a professional counselor or therapist.)

2. Read over your story as if it were someone else's and you were looking for clues, as a good detective would. Look for the basic emotion in the story, whether it's fear, anger, sadness, or some other emotion.

3. Acknowledge that you feel this way when you're challenged by this particular situation. Now it no longer has the power over you it had before. You're the one in control. You have faced the dragon and moved toward it.

4. Continue taking control of the situation by imagining yourself feeling more comfortable in the situation the next time you're in it. Imagine you're completely comfortable and happy as you see, hear, or feel yourself back there again. Ask for love and guidance from your higher Self or God. Know that you are choosing to "change the channel" on this program and do it!

Loving Your Emotional-Self Exercise
10—ADVICE TO YOURSELF

1. Write down any area(s) in your life that give you stress. It could be health, unhappiness with a job, relationships, or something else.

2. If I were my best friend who loved me dearly, what advice would I give myself? Write it down right now. You may tell a friend to see a doctor, find a new job, get out of that abusive relationship, or at least get professional help. Now make a commitment to yourself. You will never find a friend who is willing to interfere in your life enough to pick you up bodily and take you to seek health care or counseling without your consent. You must depend on yourself to be your *own* best friend when it comes to taking action in your life.

3. If you didn't do #2 because you are concerned about the cost, figure out how much you spend on clothes, automobiles, travel, and entertainment, or items to please others. Isn't your core happiness just as important? Doesn't it make sense to take care of your health and well-being first, so you have more real joy to give others?

Loving Your Emotional-Self Exercise
11—IMPROVED SELF-ESTEEM

1. Take a look at your friendships and relationships of various kinds. Ask yourself if you would treat a person the way you have been treated. If the answer is "Yes, I have been treated kindly," then skip the rest of this

exercise. If the answer is "No, I have not been treated kindly," then proceed.

2. Do you treat others kindly? Then you deserve to be treated well in return. Take a moment to think of how you might move toward other friendships and let go of the ones that do not serve you as well as you serve them.

3. Know that you will instantly improve your self-esteem by doing so. Sometimes it is the only way. For more on this, see *The Six Pillars of Self-Esteem* by Nathaniel Branden.

4. Continue until you feel it is time to stop. Trust yourself to know.

During this exercise you may feel yourself wanting to cry or write your feelings in your journal. You may even fall asleep. Let yourself do whatever comes to you. Notice how your attitudes change in relationships and how much more you rely on yourself to create the love in your life.

Loving Your Emotional-Self Exercise
12—Healing a Loss

1. Breathe deeply and relax into your body. Invite your guardian angel or spiritual teacher to be with you and guide you in this exercise daily.

2. Think of someone or something—such as a friend, child, or pet—that you love in some way other than ro-

mantically. Say the word *love* to yourself and feel the love in your heart.

3. Imagine the pain of loss or the great need for love floating up and out of your body and dispersing, like mist from a steaming pot.

4. Envision your angel or teacher with his/her hand on your heart, healing the old wound, smoothing the old scars, and making you whole. Imagine a white or golden light filling the area and feel the comfort it brings.

Loving Your Emotional-Self Exercise
13—REMOVING BLOCKS IN YOUR DREAMS

1. Write down the fear or block that you think may be getting in the way of your experiencing more love.

2. Ask God or your guardian angel for a dream that will help you better understand how to get through these blocks.

3. When you wake up, write down everything you can remember, even if it is just one word. *You* will know what it means. Trust that you will get the answer you need.

4. Repeat this dream exercise every night until you remember something. Always pick up a pen and paper in the morning, even if you remember nothing. Give this thirty days, if necessary. It can take awhile or require several dreams, if you are not ready for the answer.

LOVING YOURSELF EXERCISES FOR MAKING
LIFE CHANGES

Loving Your Life Exercise
1—LIFE ENHANCEMENT

1. Make a list here or in your personal journal of some
things you may want to improve upon.

The list can relate to anything in your life. It does
not have to require money. Remember, these are possibilities only. You are simply writing these down as
an exercise to see how they will help you and others.
You need not commit to any of it, unless you so
choose.

Use the following list as a guide, if needed, for ideas:

Money	Career
Family	Relationships
Hobbies	Clothing
Food	Education
Health	Friendships
Vacations	Fun
Adventure	Arts
Music	Entertainment
Sports	Relaxation

2. Next to the things you could possibly do for yourself,
write down whom those things may help. For example:

WHAT   **WHOM IT WILL HELP**

1. Fun—

Go to that new   Me, restaurant employees,
restaurant.   and owners, suppliers,

food manufacturers,
farmers, and so on

2. Arts—

Take a pottery class.   Me, the art school, my art
teacher, clay manufacturers,
those who receive my pots,
those who are inspired to
take an art class

As you can see, the more you do for *yourself*, the
more you automatically do for others. You can't help it!
Isn't life grand?

Here's one idea that costs absolutely nothing:

Consider making a date with yourself to see the sunset
today or tomorrow, even if you have to sneak a peek from
the window at work. Imagine it's the highest, purest love
possible coming through a special window of heaven that
opens once a day. It's there for you as well as everyone
else, because *you are part* of the one Spirit, Creator, God,
or whatever you choose to call this universal life force and
higher power that reveals itself as unconditional love.

As you watch the sun rise or set, see if you can feel
the love of God for all creation, *including you*, coming
through the light and beauty you are beholding. Feel
that love melting through any remaining walls or blocks
to love that you may have and caressing you with its
eternal flow.

Loving Your Life Exercise
2—FULFILLING BASIC NEEDS

1. Write down two or three things here, in your journal or on a slip of paper that you have needed or wanted for a while. The items could be as simple and inexpensive as a new hair barrette, brush, or comb. How about new kitchen towels or a pretty soap dispenser for the bathroom? What about that picture frame you've been meaning to get to spruce up your bedroom? Your umbrella's broken and you live in Portland, Oregon? Oh NO! Actually, that happened to me, and I bought a really nice one for two bucks at Goodwill when I was down on the dough. *You* can spend one dollar at a garage sale giving yourself a nice gift, if you're short on cash, as I was.

   _____

   _____

   _____

   _____

   _____

   _____

2. Choose one of the items on your list from #1 above and put it on your grocery list. If you need to go to a different store, DO IT. You can do it at a nearby department store or pharmacy the same day you grocery shop.

3. Thank yourself for being kind to yourself. Go home and look at your new item and grin with glee. You

have a right to enjoy everything life has to offer, no matter how simple. The more I am grateful for the little things and the more love I have in my life, the more my needs are easily filled.

4. Pat yourself on the back and realize that you have helped not only yourself, but many others. You have helped the economy by improving the wealth of those with whom you do business and those with whom *they* do business and those with whom their vendors do business, ad infinitum! It humbles me to think that loving myself becomes a gift to all of life—and it comes full circle. Being selfish can be extremely self*less*.

Loving Your Life Exercise
3—LIVING HAPPILY AND FULFILLED

1. Make a list of the things you like to do or would like to do that make you happiest. Use your journal or the space below:

_____

_____

_____

_____

_____

_____

_____

_____

_____

_____

_____

_____

_____

_____

2. Choose one thing that you would like to do, commit to it, and sign and date your commitment; then watch as miracles happen to bring it about!

_____

_____

_____

_____

_____

_____

_____date_____

3. What makes you *un*happy? Make a list. How many of these things are necessary to keep in your life? Get help from a professional therapist if what makes you unhappy is taking over your world. Imagine yourself free. What positive people, activities, things would you put in their place?

4. Choose one thing that is possible to change and make a commitment to change it by signing and dating your commitment after writing, "This will change." Forget about *how* it will change; just write it, turn it over to God, and look for life to show you what to do next. Trust yourself to know. You may be smarter than you think!

_____

_____

_____

_____

_____

_____

_____

_____

_____date_____

Loving Your Life Exercise
4—MAKING A DATE WITH YOURSELF

1. Make a date with yourself to do something you like. Be sure you have decided exactly what you want to do first, such as what movie, play, or restaurant to go to.

2. Now invite someone to go with you. Be specific about what you're going to do, so your friend is clear that this is YOUR PARTY: for example: "I'm going to my favorite restaurant for dinner and then to see the play *A Midsummer Night's Dream*. Would you like to join me?"

This way, you'll get a feel for what you want, what makes you happy inside, and what feels right to you, instead of just going along with the wishes of others when you may not really want to. Of course, compromising is very important in any relationship, but not *this* time. This particular experience is just for you, and you can explain this to your friend or family member.

Loving Your Life Exercise
5—COMMITTING TO YOURSELF

1. Like a good detective, begin looking for clues as to how you can make more of a commitment to yourself. Other people give you clues by the way they treat you. For example, perhaps someone in your life lacks the courtesy to let you know that he or she appreciates something nice you did for him or her. Write about the situation here or in your journal.

_____

_____

_____

_____

_____

_____

_____

_____

_____

_____

_____

2. Choose one key phrase to condense the feelings you have about the situation. Write the word or phrase as in the above examples: "Lack of consideration" and "No appreciation."

_____

_____

_____

3. Now ask yourself a question formed from the phrase above about how you may treat yourself this same way. Example: "How do I have a lack of consideration for myself?" or "Do I appreciate myself enough?" Write your answer here or in your journal:

_____

_____

_____

_____

_____

_____

_____

_____

4. Find a way to appreciate yourself more or be more considerate of yourself. Examples of this are buying higher quality clothing, which will actually last longer and look better; eating healthier, better quality food; paying greater attention to health care and exercise; simply smiling at yourself; and being aware that you have done a good job, no matter what anyone else says. Write your ideas here or in your journal.

_____

_____

_____

_____

_____

_____

_____

Loving Your Life Exercise
6—SAYING "NO"

If you have trouble saying "No" when you really want to, ask a friend or family member to help you practice this technique:

1. Have someone ask you for a mock favor. Example: Your friend says, "Will you drive me to the store?" or "Will you help me wash the car?"

2. Reply, "Let me think about it." Or just say, "I'm sorry; I won't be able to do that for you this time." You might also give other suggestions or suggest other people to help, if the asker seems distraught.

3. Continue saying "Let me think about that" every time someone asks you to do something, then take time to think about it. Give your real answer later, and trust that it is best for everyone concerned.

Loving Your Life Exercise
7—DOING WHAT YOU LOVE

Get out your journal, or write the answers here to these questions:

1. What makes you happy? What makes your heart sing?

_____

_____

_____

_____

_____

_____

_____

_____

_____

_____

_____

2. What would you do with your life if you had millions
   of dollars and never had to work again, ever?

_____

_____

_____

_____

_____

_____

_____

_____

_____

_____

3. What makes you feel light and good and filled with
   love?

_____

_____

_____

_____

_____

_____

_____

_____

_____

_____

_____

_____

4. What have you always dreamed of doing but never done?

_____

_____

_____

_____

_____

_____

_____

_____

_____

_____

As you look at the answers to the above questions, choose one thing you'd really love to do and decide now to look into it. You don't have to do it yet—just research the feasibility. Let yourself play with it. Go to the library and find out everything you can about it. Except for talking to experts from whom you need information, keep your idea to yourself until you see it begin to manifest itself.

Loving Your Life Exercise
8—HEART'S DESIRE

If you find yourself in a somewhat "unloving yourself" cycle of working too hard or too long:

1. Take just one day off and make a commitment to yourself to spend the entire day relaxing and writing down goals.

2. Write down goals using *Loving Your Life Exercise #7.*

3. Imagine yourself doing all of the things that you came up with, in the particular environments, using all of your senses (seeing, hearing, smelling, tasting, touching), as if you were watching a video playing in your mind.

4. When you return to work, have a chat with your boss, even if that is yourself! Ask for some time to talk about what it will take to make you the most efficient—that is, healthy and sane—employee.

5. If you are the boss, delegate! Hire someone if necessary, and don't tell me you can't afford it. My income doubled as soon as I let go of my fears and hired a part-time assistant. I had double the time to do what I am most effective doing—selling myself.

LOVING YOURSELF EXERCISES FOR YOUR SPIRITUAL SELF

Loving Your Soul Exercise
1—SELF-TRUST

1. Think and write in your journal, if you wish, of a time you trusted yourself but thought you had made a grave error. Perhaps you still think you made a mistake back then. Did you learn anything from the experience? Would you have been able to learn the lesson without the experience?

   _____

   _____

   _____

   _____

   _____

   _____

   _____

   _____

   _____

   _____

   _____

2. Who was hardest on you—yourself or your friends, family, or coworkers?

   _____

   _____

   _____

3. How did the experience help you become more of who you are today? Do you consider yourself wiser, more mature, more loving toward others than you were then? Did that experience help you reach new heights in the ability to refrain from judging others?

---

4. Confirm to yourself now that no experience is ever wasted if you learn something from it. Very likely, others learn from it too. Masters of success tell us that anyone who has never made a mistake has never tried to do anything, especially anything worthwhile.

5. Try looking at an "error" that may still be bothering you right now. Ask yourself what your best friend would say about you in that instance?

Loving Your Soul Exercise
2—DISCOVERING BLOCKS

Exercise for discovering and dissolving blocks to experiencing more love:

1. Breathe in deeply, filling your body with a warm, gentle feeling of peace and contentment in this moment.

Breathe in and out a few times, imagining a warm, glowing light filling your body from head to toe. Imagine some relaxing music you love.

2. After you read the next two parts of this exercise, close your eyes and do them. Think of a wonderful country scene—a relaxing pastoral setting where you are walking toward an old stone wall. Imagine the stone wall has a description of your "block to love" written on it. It may be a feeling rather than actual words, but the words will form themselves as you stand in front of the wall. Ask your higher Self, guardian angel, or God for guidance.

3. Imagine yourself taking down the wall, stone by stone, until it's easy for you to step over it and move on.

4. What did you see? If nothing, try again later. Now you can begin to resolve these old limits to your happiness in life. Whether you require therapy or not is up to you. You will know, if you pray, meditate, or contemplate about it. Otherwise, try this next exercise to see if you can begin to release the old fear or pain. The imagination can do wonders!

Loving Your Soul Exercise
3—CONQUERING BLOCKS

1. Imagine that the block to love you are being bothered by is a dragon with a nameplate around its neck.

2. No matter how ferocious this dragon may seem, try to realize that the power of love is much greater and that

you can turn this dragon into a kitten with the simplicity of love.

3. Begin to think of this dragon as a part of you that may be hurting, angry, or scared, like a child who has lost its way and is frightened. Imagine sending out waves of love to your dragon, the kind of love you would give your own child if she/he were lost or hurting. As you do this, you will see a change taking place.

4. Watch what happens over time as you do this exercise when you feel lost, angry, or afraid. Write what you notice in your journal. Perhaps the dragon will turn into a smaller, more manageable pet or even disappear altogether. Maybe you will be able to face these emotions and even let go of them completely in these situations. Commend yourself for your work and your progress, even if they take awhile—mine sure did!

Loving Your Soul Exercise
4—RECEIVING DIVINE LOVE

1. Begin to imagine there is love all around you. You may want to close your eyes and envision a rosy glow of light—invisible to everyone, but present just the same.

2. Feel yourself relaxing into this light, as if it had substance to hold you, just as a mother would lovingly hold her baby.

Sometimes it takes discipline, strange as that may sound, to be able to receive love. It also takes imagination.

Can you imagine that God loves *you* as much as God loves anyone else? Can you imagine that this love surrounds you always?

Set aside a special time of day—even as little as one-to-five minutes will do. Use the time to pray, meditate, sing your favorite hymn or HU, repeat a sacred phrase you cherish, or simply do the above exercise. Fill yourself with love before you begin. You can do this by thinking of someone or something you love and then letting the feeling of love take over as the images fall away. You are immersed in love! Watch your life change from this small discipline, and fill yourself with gratitude that you have made the change with your loving efforts and the help of divine guidance.

Loving Your Soul Exercise
5—ACCEPTING LOVE

1. Think of the love you have right now in your life—from parents, children, a mate, pets, friends, family, classmates, church mates, coworkers. Sometimes a smile from a stranger can bring more love than anyone you know.

2. No matter how small the amount of love, even from small compliments or courtesies, gather all of it in your mind. Then let it flow into your heart. Feel the warmth and joy of it.

3. Now imagine surrounding yourself with this love. Thank God or your own higher power for all the love in your life. Feel thankful you have the love you have, from wherever it comes.

Loving Your Soul Exercise
6—OASIS OF LOVE

Sit quietly and take a few deep breaths. Each time you breathe out, let all the tension in your body flow out. Imagine you are walking through a vast, lonely desert. You can feel the sand shifting under your feet as the sun's warmth penetrates your clothing. The only sound is the wind, which only adds to your throat's dry, parched feeling. You feel as though you are the only soul for miles upon miles. A green speck appears in front of you. It could be an oasis. You become hopeful and continue to move in the direction of the bright green area in the distance. You get close enough to see that it is indeed an oasis. As you get much closer to it, you hear the most beautiful melody on earth coming from its center.

Now imagine yourself walking into this oasis. You're struck by the beauty of the lovely white marble fountain in its center. Next to the fountain stands your guardian angel. Filled with love, light, and the music of heaven, she/he offers you a golden cup filled with liquid from this fountain. You accept it gratefully. The water is sweet and pure, more refreshing than anything you've ever drunk. You feel its magical quality filling you with the most sublime, unconditional love you have ever felt. Your angel then invites you to step into the fountain. You do so and feel completely surrounded by this love.

Know here and now that this is God's love for you and that this feeling can be gotten directly at any moment in time simply by opening your heart to it and allowing it to encompass you like a warm hug. Imagine that this is happening now.

Loving Your Soul Exercise
7—RECEIVING LOVE

1. Look into a mirror and pretend you are someone else looking at you. Imagine you're a higher being, your guardian angel, or your spiritual teacher looking into your eyes. Imagine how this being might see you when looking at you with love. The being may look deep into your eyes and see the spark of life of your true Self.

2. Say, "I love you, (your name here)." Do this every time you look into a mirror, whether silently or out loud. Notice how you feel in the days that follow.

3. To take this one step beyond, you may try imagining the voice of God saying to you, "I love you, (your name here)." Notice how this makes you feel. Do you doubt God's love for you? Do this for one week as an exercise in divine love. See how it makes you feel about yourself and others. Note your findings in your journal.

Loving Your Soul Exercise
8—FINDING YOUR GUARDIAN ANGEL

1. Before you go to sleep tonight, write a letter to God in your journal. Ask to be introduced to your guardian angel in your dreams. Leave the journal by your bed or, even better, under your pillow.

2. When you wake up, even if in the middle of the night, write down anything you can remember, no matter how silly or unrelated it may seem. Later it *will* make sense. Write down any words, even if you can only remember one. Write down any feelings. If there are no words, simply write the feelings. Perhaps you will feel filled with love or a warm embrace. Write down everything and anything.

3. Do this every day for thirty days until you have some recall.

Loving Your Soul Exercise
9—FOLLOWING YOUR HEART

Follow Your Heart

You are your own best friend.

When all others have gone,
    You alone will be there for you.

When all others have given their advice,
    You alone will be left with the results of
      your decision.

When every ear has turned to hear another,
    You alone will be there to listen to yourself.

Sometimes your outer circumstances appear to warrant certain decisions that your loved ones encourage you to make. Common sense tells you to make those decisions, but your heart and soul guide you in a different direction. If you know it is your highest Self and your true purpose, follow what you know in your heart that you need and want from life. Can you love yourself enough to give it to yourself?

Starting a Think Yourself Loved Support Group

SOMETIMES THOSE OF US who have had to struggle with loving ourselves more find solace in knowing we are not alone. If you feel the desire to share your triumphs, ideas, and discoveries with others, think about beginning a support group.

A support system can be as simple as you and your best friend talking once a week about your progress, cheering each other on, and discussing new ideas. That's exactly how I came up with the idea of loving myself—by talking with a friend about it for a few months, then continuing on my own.

A support group can also be one led by your therapist

or minister, and this would be advisable if there are deep emotional issues to be dealt with in the group. Ask, and I am sure you will find someone willing.

I'm certain you'll find others just as thirsty for this kind of gathering as you are. Let's talk about who might want to be part of a *Think Yourself Loved* support group. See if you relate to any of these reasons for someone wanting to join such a group (or to work with friends on this):

- Needing to feel you're not the only one.
- Knowing there's strength in numbers.
- Wanting to speed up the process.
- Knowing that others have good ideas you may need or want to use.
- Wanting the reinforcement of watching others' success.
- Getting the encouragement and cheers of others for your success.
- Wanting to be of service in helping others with this process.
- Realizing how much you have to offer to others, just by being yourself!

BUILDING YOUR OWN SUPPORT GROUP

To make it simple and easy for you to begin a support group, I've listed the following steps. Begin with a positive attitude and things will go well. Think of how much love you will be helping bring into other people's lives and what a great service that will be. You will benefit greatly if you decide to lead the group, since we often learn best by teaching!

Step 1 —Set a Goal

Set a written goal for the kind of group you want. Include the number of people, the atmosphere, the time of day, and the place you'd like to meet. I'd suggest limiting your meetings to one hour. Also, write the desired number of sessions you'd like for the group. If you meet once a week, I would recommend having no more than eight sessions, then asking the group whether they would like to continue after that. If you meet only monthly, you could extend the group to one year and it would not be too much for people.

Step 2 —Find a Space and Interested People

Use your imagination to create a wonderful group in a wonderful space. Then use your common sense to think of the best alternative that is cost-free or very low in cost, to allow everyone's participation. Check with your church or local chamber of commerce for ideas, or ask if anyone is willing to share his or her home for the sessions. You may also want to alternate homes among the group members.

Ask your friends, church mates, or health club members if they know anyone who would be interested. Some bookstores have space and will advertise in their newsletters for you. Church bulletins may do the same. It's fine if just two people are interested. It's just as healing with two as with ten. I'd suggest no more than twelve to fifteen to a group. You can always encourage a new group to begin if there are too many people.

Step 3—SET AN INITIAL MEETING DATE

Decide when to have a first meeting to consider all the rest of the meeting basics, such as where and when you will continue and what you will ask for a fee or donation (I would suggest that $3—$5 a person for each session could be donated to the church, school, bookstore, or other meeting place or that the money could be spent on other learning tools to share, if in someone's home).

Decide how often you'd like to meet and who will lead the sessions (or whether you will alternate among the group). Please note that in this chapter there is a simple outline to follow so that anyone may lead the group. You can take turns being the group leader so that everyone learns more.

In the first meeting I'd also recommend asking members what they feel the goal is for them personally and for the group so you may work toward a common end.

TOOLS FOR LEADING A SUPPORT GROUP

Tool 1 —CREATE A POSITIVE ATMOSPHERE

Always start on a positive, happy note and be sure everyone in the group knows this is vital. It helps to lay a comfortable, safe, and trusting foundation for people to open their hearts, for sharing their true thoughts and feelings.

Of course, people will have sadness or anger at times over certain experiences, and these are perfectly valid. The way to bring the group back to a positive outlook is to allow those feelings to be expressed and then ask the person how he or she resolved the situation or plans to resolve the situation, if it is still occurring. The main idea is to stay with the thought that we *do* have control of our own lives and that we are the only ones who do.

Tool 2—LISTEN TO EVERYTHING WITH AN OPEN HEART

Listen. Listen. Listen. I know this can be difficult, especially if you relate to the other person's experience and you're sure you know just how to fix it. How do I know? I have, of course, given lots of advice when I could have just listened and let the person come to his or her own conclusions. I learned to ask the right questions, such as "What do *you* think would be the best solution?" If you must say something, ask questions or talk about your own experiences without telling anyone else what to do.

Make sure everyone in the group knows that it is safest to simply listen, unless someone specifically asks the group for help or ideas. Most people will answer their own questions and learn much more that way, if simply given the freedom to talk to an open-minded listener.

Tool 3—USE JOURNALS

Ask each member of the group to bring a journal to each meeting. You may want to provide journals that were purchased using funds from the meeting fees.

The journal acts as a sounding board for each group member to relay private thoughts and feelings during the discussion. Some people may be hesitant to talk at first, or ever, due to personality and experiential differences. The journal gives them the opportunity to express themselves without talking and risking being judged, criticized, or advised.

Other uses for journals are to create a better understanding of certain experiences with the perspective that is provided by writing over time, to chart progress and realizations during the escape from old thoughts and beliefs, and to make commitments on paper via personally written contracts.

Tool 4—Stick With the Topic

The support group members are there because they have a need to resolve blocks to loving themselves, and they are serious about moving ahead. In order to keep the class on track, as the facilitator it is your responsibility to notice if someone seems to be straying from the subject of people thinking themselves loved. As lovingly as you can, say something like this: "Perhaps we can discuss that after our meeting, since we're limited on time for our topic."

Tool 5—Ask Group Members to Read This Book Thoroughly First

If everyone in the group is working from the same assumptions, your meetings will run much more smoothly. This book is a starting point from which to begin discussions. You will each have your own ideas to share and wonderful new Loving Yourself Exercises to use. Pool your ideas and thoughts about how you may best utilize the in-

formation presented here, based upon your common beliefs and studies. If you are a church group, use your holy
scriptures or teachings to support your process and
choose what works well with that from this book.

𝑇ool 6—Use an Outline for Leading the Group

Now you are ready to begin. The following outline
will help you get started. The structure is simply a suggestion. If you are a therapist, minister, or professional
counselor, you may feel the need to update this or
change it to meet the needs of your congregants or
clients. Please feel free to utilize it in the most positive
way you can imagine.

1. *Ask all attendees to share the positive experiences
   with thinking themselves loved* that they had during
   the week or since you last met. Invite all to discuss the
   positive results of the homework assignment. Ask
   them to record these experiences in their journals, if
   they have not already done so.

2. *Ask all to write and discuss,* if comfortable, present
   concerns, setbacks, guilts, hesitations, or fears about
   loving themselves more and giving to themselves in
   the way described in the homework exercise. If someone has a concern that doesn't fit with the homework,
   but is still about the subject of people thinking themselves loved, certainly listen.
   Ask people who are verbally expressive about some
   of these issues to say what they would do to resolve

them if they could love themselves more. Ask them to write these down.

3. *Bring out one new principle to be discussed for today's meeting.* This could be from the assigned homework. Ask the attendees how they plan to apply this new principle or how they have done so already.

4. *Do a creative exercise* using that same principle. It can be from this book or one you or a group member have developed. Do the exercise now for practice, writing or role-playing if it fits the exercise. Some people may wish to discuss the results of the exercise, if time allows.

5. *Assign homework.* Assign the above exercise to the group to do at least once before the next meeting or to practice once a day, if appropriate. Ask them to jot down the results to share next week at the beginning of the meeting. Assign a portion of a chapter to contemplate and work with in their daily lives, writing down any realizations. Ask them to think of a different creative exercise to do with it as well, if they would like.

6. *End on a positive note* of expectation for new progress next week or month in each person's efforts to become a happier, more loving person.

❤ ❤ ❤

A support group of this nature can be an enjoyable learning experience. Many people form lasting friendships and find a new approach to all areas of their lives. Leading a group such as this can boost your own efforts tenfold.

Here's to your continued success in loving yourself and loving others!

Bibliography

Anderson, Linda C., *35 Golden Keys to Who You Are & Why You're Here*, Eckankar, Minneapolis, 1997.

Branden, Nathaniel, *The Six Pillars of Self-Esteem*, Bantam, New York, 1994.

Fillmore, Charles, *The Revealing Word*, Unity Books, Unity Village, Missouri, 1997.

Finley, Guy, *The Secret of Letting Go*, Llewellyn Publications, St. Paul, Minnesota, 1990.

Johnson, Debbie, *Think Yourself Thin*, Hyperion, New York, 1996.

Weiner-Davis, Michele, *Fire Your Shrink!*, Simon & Schuster, New York, 1995.

SUGGESTED READING

Butterworth, Eric, *In the Flow of Life*, Unity Books, Unity Village, Missouri, 1994.

Dyer, Dr. Wayne W., *You'll See It When You Believe It*, Morrow, New York, 1989.

Moore, Mary Carroll, *How to Master Change in Your Life*, Eckankar, Minneapolis, 1997.

SUGGESTED LISTENING

Amos, Wally, *Let Go, Let God* (cassette), Unity Multimedia, Unity Village, Missouri, 1998.

Klemp, Harold, *HU: A Love Song to God*, Eckankar, Minneapolis, 1990.

ORDERING OTHER DEBBIE JOHNSON WORKS

To order copies of Debbie Johnson's *Think Yourself Thin* book or audio or video cassette or a copy of her booklet *How to Make Your Dreams Come True*, call 1-800-600-3483.

About the Author

DEBBIE JOHNSON NEVER WANTED TO WRITE A BOOK, but somehow it happened, with an inner nudge from Spirit. She's now written several and continues to write, because she must.

Johnson originally published all her own books, and did what everyone told her was impossible: live on her income from self-publishing. Having met and overcome many challenges to success, Debbie's ultimate goal is helping others make their dreams come true.

Living in Minneapolis with her husband Myron Cheshaek, Debbie says their two cats have taught her much about loving and taking care of herself. She enjoys dancing; natural gourmet health-food cooking; and volunteering for her church, Eckankar, the religion of the light and sound of God. She loves exploring the ways the Holy Spirit works in dreams and everyday life, from health to career to simple day-to-day tasks.